A WESTERN DOCTOR'S ODYSSEY
FROM CARIBOO TO KOS

ELDON LEE

HERITAGE HOUSE

Canadian Cataloguing in Publication Data
Lee, Eldon 1923-
A western doctor's odyssey

ISBN 1-895811-21-X

1. Lee, Eldon, 1923-   2. Physicians—British Columbia—
Hazelton—Biography.   3. Hazelton (B.C.)—Biography.   I. Title.
R464.L44A3 1996   610'.92   C96-910635-1

First Edition

Heritage House wishes to acknowledge the ongoing support its publishing program receives from Heritage Canada, the Cultural Services Branch of the BC Government and the BC Heritage Trust.

Edited by Antonia Banyard
Cover, Book Design, and Typesetting by Cecilia Hirczy Welsford

Heritage House Publishing Company Limited
#8 – 17921 55 Avenue, Surrey BC V3S 6C4

Printed in Canada

DEDICATED TO MARJORIE

One ever ready to start a new adventure and never flinching from sacrifices for her husband, family and the profession of medicine which has demanded so much of us. To you, my loving wife, mother of our six children, sojourner with me on the many paths of life, I give my thanks and my love.

Ave Always, your husband
Eldon

CONTENTS

INTRODUCTION

The Cariboo referred to in the title of this book is that distinctive part of central British Columbia around the community of Williams Lake. More specifically, during adolescence, my Cariboo revolved around the Hill and Paul Ranch south-east of that town. While the Cariboo and the magnificent lands on its periphery have played a very tangible role in my life, Kos as a destination, is more abstract. Kos is a Greek island in the Aegean Sea, the birthplace 2500 years ago of Hippocrates, the father of modern medicine.

The geographical distance from Cariboo to Kos symbolizes the lengthy journey of a western ranch lad en route to becoming a renowned consultant in the specialty of obstetrics and gynaecology.

In this image, found on the east wall of the College of Physicians in Vancouver, BC, Hippocrates of Kos holds a Caduceus, the symbol of the medical profession. The father of modern medicine was born on the Greek Island of Kos in 460 BC.

PREFACE

"Doctor, lawyer, merchant, chief...." This old nursery rhyme presents the dilemma which young people face the world over and in all times: that of choosing a profession. As a boy I dreamed of being a garbage man, then a flyer, a farmer, and a fireman. Riches, power, or influence were not priorities.

The real events of my life exceeded my wildest dreams. I could not have imagined the wonders in store.

These dreams were far removed as I struggled through a rather tumultuous upbringing on an isolated cattle ranch in the Cariboo country of British Columbia. Because of the isolation, my brother Todd and I were taught at home, from elementary school through high school. In our free time, we participated fully in chores and, when we were old enough, worked very hard from early morning until evening cutting wood, repairing fences, or riding the range, watching over our horses and cattle.

We had a loving, supportive family — mother and grandparents, although fragmented with the absence of a father. We had encouragement to study and dream, and we were made to feel that God had a purpose and course laid out for us, even though Grandma in exasperation would sometimes refer to us as "young limbs of the devil." As one might gather, our home was quite religious.

We considered ourselves missing many of the good things of life. Little did we realize that we had a full measure of the great things.

Still, while growing up in central British Columbia, half a world distant from the Greek isle of Kos, the birthplace of Hippocrates, I did not envision advanced university degrees and a distinguished role in the professions of medicine and humanities. These and many other honours were to be mine; truly, my journey was a modern odyssey.

CHAPTER 1

INTRODUCTION TO THE HEALING ARTS

Our family was not inclined to medicine; there were many farmers, lawyers, workers, ministers, and soldiers, but as far as I know only one doctor, a distant cousin. I did, however, inherit a healing touch from my mother, who had a talent for making people feel better, both physically and mentally. My younger brother Todd was also a sensitive and caring person, who felt the woes of others so keenly that it adversely affected his life. My mother kept a better balance, although she did not have the awful weight of direct responsibility that later fell on Todd and me in our professions. By nature I was halfway between my mother and Todd. I was sensitive, but tough mentally and physically.

My healing role began when, at eight years of age, I assumed the guardian role of looking after Todd. It happened that at night he would become croupy with coughing and wheezing, which may have been a type of asthma. My response was to stoke up the fire in the big pot-bellied stove and boil water, then steam him thoroughly with a mentholated ointment.

In other ways I took the brunt of the blame for my younger brother. On one occasion we were into some mischief and it was Todd who erred. When the mischief was discovered I was blamed, and Todd, the guilty one, came away scot-free. I remember retaliating by filling my rubber boot with water and, from the vantage point of a corner of the machine shop, waiting until he came down the path. I threw the full boot at him, and for my pains received another scolding. Such an event was rare, so rare in fact that I still remember it.

Opposite: Eldon Lee, a serious young MD, Hazelton, BC, 1959.

On another occasion I may have saved Todd from drowning. We had just taught ourselves to swim and ventured to a deep hole in the creek adjacent to our cattle ranch. Todd waded in, and soon over his head, he immediately forgot what little swimming knowledge he had. Bobbing up and down in the pool, he sank deeper with each submersion. I dove into the pool and after pushing him towards safety immediately went under the surface myself, swallowing water and choking. Fortunately the pool was only about ten feet across, and I was able to extricate myself and find Todd near the shoreline choking and coughing from the water that he had inhaled. We threw our arms around each other for a moment, then, naked as we were born, trotted along the creek to find more excitement.

In our teen years, Todd's abilities seemed to lie in the mechanical field, and mine in the welfare of our cattle and horses. I found that I was able to walk beside mean-minded and wild horses without their taking alarm. It was only the tamer horses that I was familiar with, that kicked, bit, or struck me.

At one time, several of our horses were infected with the disease called fistula, a festering lesion of the withers. Treating this required that the horse be thrown onto its side and the deep fistulous tract washed out with hydrogen peroxide and then a phenol solution. This usually required daily treatments for up to eight weeks.

Barbed wire was a constant bane of ranchers, as cattle and horses were forever getting tangled in it and sustaining lacerations. When deep enough, these had to be sutured with black silk thread. On occasion this too required throwing the animal. Later on as a surgeon I found this early experience in suturing to be of value in fine hand movements.

My future fastidiously clean patients may not have been thrilled, had they known that my first maternity experience came in the animal world. Sometimes cows developed obstetrical problems when calving, and the rancher assumed the role of the *accoucheur* or midwife. The usual complications were malpositions or retained afterbirths. The solution was to tie the unfortunate cow to something secure, take off one's shirt, wash hands and arms, reach in, and straighten the calf out or remove the afterbirth.

On one memorable occasion, I found a heifer whose calf was firmly stuck with its nose directed awry. A rope was placed around the heifer's neck, and she was tied to a tree in the approved fashion. It was a snowy day with the temperature below freezing, but I took

Top: In 1931, two transplanted California boys, Todd and Eldon (right) Lee take up residence on a remote Cariboo ranch.

Bottom Left: Mother and relentless teacher, Shirley Lee poses with her two star pupils.

Bottom Right: Eldon Lee as Cariboo teenager on the Hill and Paul Ranch with "Tony".

off my coat, shirt, and undershirt, scrubbed my hands and arms in the snow, went in, and straightened the calf out for delivery.

One advantage to veterinary medicine is that if the treatment fails, one can always dispatch the patient. This is not an option for a physician.

Certain things in ranching folklore which proved effective defied logical explanation. It was a practice when a horse had an infected hoof to place the foot in a gunny sack filled with soft cow manure. To me, this seemed to be exactly the wrong treatment, but it did work. Later in medical school, I found out that cow manure teems with coliform bacteria, which are the sworn enemy of streptococci and staphylococci, the common cause of infected foot lesions. I suspect that many other folk remedies have just as sound a basis for their effectiveness.

While there were inclinations toward medicine through the years, I established no firm resolve. It was not until I was in grade 12 of our home school that I developed the equipment for the study of medicine. It was at that time that my intellect expanded in a quantum leap, and my IQ was measured at the genius level. There seemed to be a conscious letting loose of the perimeters of my mind, and a tremendous hunger for mental growth followed. Over threescore years I have retained the capacity for recollection of infinite detail. I am completely unable to explain this growth, and to this day I am not sure what happened. I wish I could share the ability to recollect details with my children, but perhaps it is something that individuals must learn for themselves.

Be that as it may, I graduated from the Hill and Paul ranch prepared for the life that lay before me, first as a bomber pilot in the Royal Canadian Air Force and then in academic fields.

CHAPTER 2

His Majesty's Royal Canadian Flying Corps —Airplanes and Women

I had graduated from our "Hill and Paul High School" at age eighteen, wrote my matriculation, and like most other healthy young men in that era, went off to war. This was in 1943 and I was a pink-cheeked neophyte with down on my face and no experience with airplanes — even less with women. Still, for some reason, I had a yen to "have at the Hun," and being adverse to marching in any form, I joined the flying corps direct from the rural tranquility of the Hill and Paul Ranch. So it came that I stood awkwardly before my pilot counsellor in this new career.

"Dear boy," said he, "flying has to do with two things, airplanes and women. Airplanes are a bother, but we manage to cope." Puffing reflectively on his pipe he continued, "Morale is the important thing, eight nimble fingers, and two nippy thumbs, absolutely top notch. Remember that, if sex should rear its ugly head."

My mother, with the trepidation that all mothers felt at seeing a son depart for the war, had given me a few useful instructions. Not, it would seem, to protect me from the Germans in combat, but to give me some guidance in my relationship with the fairer sex.

"Dear son," said she, "at home you have led a protected life and the women that you have come in contact with have been of the highest moral character and conduct. It may be that in your flying career you may meet young women who can only be termed as 'fast.' It is important for you in your young life to avoid this type of woman. Seek one who dresses modestly, wears her hair sensibly, reads edifying literature such as Mr Dickens and Mr Bulwer Lytton; a young woman whose energies are expended in wholesome activities such as knitting and sewing."

"Very sensible," said I, "but I dare say that in the thick of the air battle, I will have little opportunity to meet any female, fast or slow."

So much for preparation for the struggle. A creature of the lowest rank, I was admitted to the Air-Arm of the Royal Canadian Air Force (RCAF) in February of 1943 and dispatched to the frozen prairies with the bloody war far away. I saw no airplanes, but received my share of battle preparation in the form of marching and washing dishes. And two memorable occurrences shaped later events.

The first was a dutiful lecture from the medical officer on the terrors of sexually-transmitted diseases. One hundred hopeful aircrew gathered together and were given a forty minute graphic lecture which left us white, pale, and shaken as we staggered out.

The second event following approximately a week after this vivid description featured our first casualty. A new recruit by the name of Erickson appeared one morning looking very contrite and shamefully confessed that shortly after the lecture he had enjoyed an evening with a wonderful young woman, and he had noted evidence of what was known as "a dishonourable discharge." Much to his sorrow the discharge was indeed dishonourable, and Erickson was left only to mutter, "She told me that I was her first real boyfriend."

Erickson disappeared from our midst but we soon heard he re-mustered into the army. Re-mustering into the army meant the infantry, where he dragged his rifle through the mud of Italy for two years while "Gerry" did his utmost to render him into a reasonable facsimile of Swiss cheese. It must rank as one of the worst complications of a sexually transmitted disease in the annals of medicine.

Several months went by with no progress at "having at the Hun" in an airplane. In spite of Erickson's fate I did notice increased activity among the air crew in "having at" local members of the female establishment. It would appear that about ten percent of the air crew could be classed as inveterate and irredeemable skirt chasers, and a surprising number of these were the married men in our midst. Young downy-cheeked recruits such as myself were too shy and inex-perienced to have any deep involvement and could only surmise. Indeed, the righteous man dreams of what the wicked man does!

Six months after enlistment, I was finally introduced to a genuine airplane. Oh, glorious day when we lined up in a field near Prince Albert, Saskatchewan with a cold wind blowing and sixty airplanes lined up before sixty eager pilots-to-be.

Pilot Eldon Lee, 1943 poses in his first airplane, a Tigermoth. "Those were the days my friend," he fondly recalls.

In ensuing days my main endeavour was to keep from being trampled by another fearless pilot who had as little skill as myself. However, I could not help but notice one of the girl mechanics who spun the propellers to start each plane. She was gloriously attractive and obviously possessed all those womanly hormones in which I was developing a keen interest.

As she walked along the line and spun propellers, I sat entranced, hoping against hope that she would direct herself to my plane.

One brisk day it happened. There she was, a picture of beauty, cheeks pink from the Saskatchewan wind, lips full, breasts shapely, full figured. I sat stunned and enraptured.

She gave a thumbs up, meaning she was ready to start the plane, and I replied with a weak thumbs up, totally entranced by this lovely face before me.

She spun the propeller and nothing happened. She tried again and again but the plane absolutely refused to start. Finally, after minutes, while I sat in the airplane gazing at this beautiful creature, she gave up in disgust and went to get the head mechanic.

At this time, awakened from my reverie, I noted with horror that I had forgotten to turn the switches on, of course denying the engine any chance of igniting. Silently, I corrected my oversight. The mechanic gave one twist to the propeller and the motor roared to life, and he muttered, "Women, they're impossible."

Being craven as I was, I had not the courage to confess. However, I did carry a red rose in my helmet for the next two weeks, but the beauteous little girl on the line never came back to my airplane.

1944 opened on a sombre event as we buried four of our fellows, after a mid-air crash, but we were heartened to know that having learned to fly airplanes as airplanes, we would now learn to fly them as weapons. Bestowed with new airplanes which were faster and heavier, our responsibilities grew greater. And we found ourselves in a different mix of comrades. For the first time we had "WD" or Women's Division members with us, and we also had a crew of RAF trainees plus veterans re-mustered from the fighting in Britain. The WDs were known as "W do's" and "W don'ts" and the category in which any woman aircrew fell was soon noted.

The RAF boys seemed to be both overeager and highly sexed. They all had endless tales to recount of sky battles, foreign places, and exotic experiences.

One man in particular stood out — Warrant Officer Harvey. He was certifiably mad, insane, bonkers, out of control and all the rest. In 1940 he had found himself on a fighter base in England, and after only ten hours in a Spitfire, was sent out to do battle.

It was likely thought he would fly wingman for a mission or two while a real pilot shot down German aircraft, then he would be made into mincemeat by some German 109 fighter. However, much to the brass's surprise, he not only survived the encounter, but excelled in it, and vowed never to forget who prematurely placed him amid the thick of battle. For the next two years he was a thorn in the flesh of the brass who had planned his sacrifice just to buy a little time.

At length it was decided in England that the battle against the German air force would proceed to victory more quickly if Warrant Officer Harvey was far away. On short notice he was transferred from fighter command to bomber command and sent back to Canada for further training.

It was obvious to us Canadians that he was absolutely mad, a judgement verified when, entrusted to marching a squad of WDs, he marched them into a fence and left them milling there, while he went off for a beer in the canteen.

Replacing my Tiger Moth this Harvard AT6 became a large part of my life.

The Women's Division hut was directly across the road from our own quarters, and one night near one o'clock there came a terrible uproar, with lights flashing and police cars gathering around. Word spread that someone had dashed headlong into the women's dormitory and turned over every bed along an entire wall, spilling the occupant onto the floor.

There was immediate suspicion in the squadron as to who might be the culprit, but Harvey lay sleeping in bed like an angel. Only a few men noticed that shoes were still on his feet.

Finally order was restored and everyone went to sleep. Two hours later the whole scene was repeated! Sirens went off, lights came on, policemen engulfed the place, and screams resounded from the women's barracks.

Provoking renewed irritation, the assailant had reappeared and turned over beds on the opposite side of the hut. There was no further sleep in either barracks for the rest of the night.

The culprit was never found, but Warrant Officer Harvey soon disappeared from our midst, and someone said they bumped into him later in Alaska. With Harvey, it seems brass everywhere resorted to the same solution.

The WDs were mostly respectable young women in uniform, and I would say that about ten percent, roughly the same percentage as pilots, were bed hoppers.

There was a tall, angular, young, uniformed woman in administration who came to my attention because she frequently accompanied one of my squadron mates to the laundry shack, located immediately back of our barracks. At the time, I thought it most unusual but commendable that someone should help a variety of my poor mates find their lost laundry.

This went on night after night, whetting my curiosity. Finally, never having such a laundry problem myself, I inquired as to how so much lost laundry kept airwoman Smythe busy every night. There were a few smirks, and I was told that airwoman Smythe's role in the war was to maintain morale and relieve tension among the pilots. Later I found out that her nickname was "Rosie the Riveter."

In our own squadron there were three worthies: Tits, Balls-up, and Horse McGeachie, all so named for obvious reasons.

Tits, right in the middle of a first class war, got married, and from that point on, he seemed to lose all interest in the battlefield. From the military perspective this may lend some truth to Kipling's words, "You may carve it on his tombstone, you may mark it on his card, but a good man married is a good man marred."

Balls-up was so called after the providential muscular reflex which Nature provided in men to maintain the continuity of the human race. When men are in a stressful situation, as in a fight, exerting maximum effort, the cremasteric muscles elevate the testicles out of harm's way. Balls-up had a steady girlfriend at home and his name bore no association with local females, but he did give his squadron the maximum effort in the air.

Not so Horse McGeachie, a legendary figure in regard to sexual prowess. One event alone established him as a legend.

Ordinarily we flew seven days a week, but on rare occasions we would be given a twenty-four-hour free period, at which time those who had some of their monthly pay left over might engage a companion and hotel room. Thus it was with McGeachie. Saturday night found him tucked in with a little popsie in the upper-floor honeymoon suite of the best hotel in Brandon.

At seven o'clock in the morning, there was a rap on the door and a female voice, "Jimmy, is that you dear?" McGeachie, waking up, exclaimed to himself, "Yoiks, it's the mater," and to his popsie, "Quick, up, into the closet." He opened the door and guided her into the laundry chute. There were shrieks of rage and indignation from below, and as McGeachie gathered purse and unmentionables to send down after their owner, he murmured softly, "Bombs away, my dear."

It was generally felt by the squadron that McGeachie's reaction time and conduct in a dicey situation was commendable, but that his performance fell short of fitting him with the Distinguished Flying

Cross. Still the event established a legend in the squadron, particularly his "Bombs away, my dear", which must rank with Rhett Butler's "Frankly my dear..."

As we proceeded with our training, a certain tenseness crept into the group. We finished our heavy duty flying, went through operational training, and, in Quebec, prepared for embarkation. I suspect I know why Pierre Trudeau, who avoided military service, exhibited disdain for Canada's armed forces. It was retaliation for wartime deals done by Western lads. Quebec girls simply loved pilots, and no girl between the age of sixteen and twenty-five would accept anyone by choice as a beau but an air force pilot.

And then one night it happened. Temptation came into my own life. She was sweet. It was eleven o'clock, and sitting on the sofa close to her, enchanted by a hauntingly seductive perfume, I was conscious that my nineteen years of living and eighteen months of intensive flying training had not equipped me to feel in command in this situation, particularly when she snuggled up and kissed me under the ear and ran a rather shapely ankle over my knee.

"Tell me, mon beau," she said, "what makes you so brave, so fearless. Why would such a fine pilot come to protect me from 'les boches'? Me, so young, so inexperienced, a simple maiden like putty in the hands of one so worldly and wise."

"It is true that I am a great pilot," I said modestly, "and the reason, of course, is that I am very meticulous in checking everything."

"Ah," she said, "perhaps you can help me with a minor dilemma. Do you think that perhaps my garter is a little bit too low?" And she flipped her flimsy shift, which seemed to know no direction but up.

What was I to think about the devastatingly tempting scarlet garter with the tiny bow on her thigh — and to my mind about as high as any garter ought to go. I was very near to the promised land, I'm sure, especially when she whispered, "Mon beau aviateur, do you not think such an insignificant ribbon should be placed a little higher?"

My mind raced. Could this be one of the "fast women" of which my mother warned? In a lightning flash I thought again of the parameters of a respectable lady. Was she modest in dress? Well, hardly any clothing at all. What about womanly pursuits such as embroidery or knitting? There was no knitting evident, and loosening my regulation tie counted for little. Edifying reading? Not a Bible could be seen, nor were Mr Bulwer Lytton's works anywhere about.

Modest hair styling? This could be positive — perhaps one out of four? Surely a passing mark.

Rescue, however, came from an entirely unexpected direction. The base's emergency siren blew a tremendous wailing blast. "Alors!" cried I, "I must get back to the base." I leaped up and bounced Simone (or was it Marie?) on the floor on her petite derriere, seized my coat, and dashed for the door.

"Duty calls, au revoir!"

There were screams: "Fou, idiot, cochon! Verdammte anglais!"

I could see that she was most distraught by the parting, but the stern discipline of a pilot's life imparts its own agenda. Alas, I was to see her no more.

We were at embarkation, and it was while there that I made an observation which I still believe is true. Young men in a combat mode are not very much into female relationships. They are on edge, tense, mean, and physically violent. There were many arguments and fights.

At the last minute it fell to my lot to not "have at the Hun" after all. I went to a base in the west, Sea Island at Vancouver. It was a dream posting with my ultimate destination being the Far East. The rest of the squadron spent the next year in the mud of Yorkshire, and there a few were buried.

A different lot fell to the RAF boys who left and were fast-tracked into battle. On a badly planned raid "Gerry" fell upon them from above. They were decimated. Alas for my squadron mates Hetherington, James, Cato, Nobby, Knowles, Jestico, and the others. In a moment their promise and potential was gone forever. This old flyboy cannot but wistfully hope that in some idealistic Canadian young woman a seed may have been planted that would extend the biologic lineage of these more or less courageous pilots.

What was to be learned from my RCAF years? Several things were of benefit later on in medicine. A looming battlefield did not change sexual practices. Education probably had little impact either. Most pilots had reasonable attitudes toward women. However, about ten percent were openly randy, seeking, soliciting and preoccupied by their own brand of conquest at all times.

In my own case and others, the attitudes and teachings imparted from home were powerful determinants in our conduct with women, and inexperience itself may also be a virtue.

Pilot Officer Lee has fond memories of Quebec. Joyce, on left, and Marie, on right, were part of "those days." As the popular war ballad said, "I thought they'd never end."

Finally, aircrew can be tense, mean, and violent; this is something to think about when introducing women into this role. The main enemy may not be in front but behind. The Greek philosopher Plato recommended to his peers that women be placed in a combat role about 2400 years ago. He barely escaped the debate with his life, and the role of women in combat is still a principle not widely established.

There it is. The war ended. The pilots came home to humdrum jobs, and the virtue of Canadian women was preserved in perpetuity I think, I trust, I hope, or was it?

CHAPTER 3

1944, 1400 Hours, August 10

In 1944 I was in RCAF aircrew, a pilot in a long stream of bomber pilots making their way towards England. After eighteen months with action as far away as ever, I felt detached, emotionally flat, and I was no longer bonded to the war. If there was any bonding, it was to my daily flying mates.

William Yeats's lines, written of a pilot, were mine:
"Those that he fights he does not hate
Those that he guards he does not love"

However, an event, lasting only a few moments, forever changed me. It was during an operational training exercise aloft above a broad expanse of Canadian prairie, and the time was 1400 hours, August 10, 1944.

Davis leaned over from his right hand seat, and his face was white.

"Ormiston's in trouble."

I looked quickly through the left window but could see no damage. True, Ormiston had strayed out about 100 feet from the usual position, tight on my left wingtip, but the propellers reflected shining circles in the afternoon sunlight, and he maintained speed.

I looked past Davis to the other wingman keeping a position tight in the V and then quickly back to my left. Ormiston's aircraft staggered, and in horror I looked along the fuselage. Almost the entire tail section was missing. Only a shattered remnant of fabric and wire trailed behind.

He was having difficulty keeping control. The aircraft plunged in awkward dips and surges. Ormiston, the happy jokester of the mess, forever contemplating a jug or a doll, was not joking now. He was fighting for his life. We could see the tenseness reflected in the movements of the brown helmet and saw his hand move to the hand trim, a fatal manoeuver.

Like a wounded animal his aircraft rose in a steep climb.

With fascination we followed in position, until he stalled and fell off into a tight spin. Down his ship went, tighter and tighter grew the circles of the wings. The plane plunged down, down.

In agony we looked for the puffs of parachutes opening. There were none.

"God, put an end to this," we cried, and from far below came a cloud of dust, a puddle of flame, and a tower of black smoke.

The two remaining aircraft crept on alone across an eternity of space. Time slowed to a standstill. Ormiston was dead.

This was the reality, and we felt the sorrow and loss more acutely later, as we watched the MPs strip his bed and pack his clothes.

Ormiston's final flight.

We had seen death, and in our minds we had experienced that last split second before our own impact. Paradoxically, there came a calmness and assurance that has remained with me. The menace of death no longer held us in its grip. Ormiston, had joined that first warrior of eons before, but, we would all have our time.

Yeats continues:

"Nor law nor duty bade me fight
 No public men nor cheering crowds
 A lonely impulse of delight
 Drove to this tumult in the clouds."

Would there ever be a last warrior? No, never in the world. The human psyche is bonded to war. Peace exists only within oneself.

CHAPTER 4

University —
A Time For Decision

Once the war had ended, I was granted an honourable discharge from the air force. It was then time for making peace. I lay down arms and took up the implements of cattle ranching with my brother Todd who had remained at the family ranch, deemed an "essential worker" by the government. After two years, rural activities became tedious. I remember 1948 as a critical year in my choice of a vocation. My career as a bomber pilot ended with the surrender of the Japanese and Germans. My academic career had halted after finishing Grade 12 and now, with the establishment of the Lazy Lee, a 1,000-acre ranch demanding endless energy and resources, ranching had lost its glamour.

My personal life presented somewhat of a dilemma also. I was seriously involved with two young ladies, one from my air force days, and one from the Williams Lake area. Both were charming and loving, and both had accepted my fervent vows of everlasting devotion, subject to terminating my association with the other. Delightful as they were, for the life of me I couldn't decide to spend my life with either one. I was not a trifler of women's tender affections, but simply did not have the maturity for marriage.

I remembered the days in the air force. Then there was a solution to problems such as these; one simply asked to be transferred to another air force base. In my present circumstances, I could not transfer to another ranch, so the problem seemed to have no immediate solution. That is, there was no immediate solution until one day a serendipitous event occurred. A stupid cow caught its leg behind a log and fractured the lower bones. Using 2 x 4-inch boards on both sides of the broken leg as a splint, I applied plaster and managed to put a respectable cast on the fractured leg, and it eventually healed. The thought occurred to me that I was gifted in the healing arts, and there had to be a better way to practice this skill than applying casts to a cow's leg.

A firm resolution came to me, and I made the decision that I would become a doctor of medicine; not a doctor of veterinary medicine, but a doctor of the noble art of healing fellow men and women who were in distress. I would bring the miracles of modern medicine to the multitudes!

This was in April, and in the next four months, the meadows were cultivated and hay piled in stacks. In September at age twenty-five I registered in Seattle Pacific College and began the first semester of pre-medical study. (Todd had already completed his freshman year in arts and continued on at the same college.) I found that I had a talent for study, and the IQ tests showed a level of 155, which was a cause for considerable comment in academic circles.

Thus encouraged and comforted by my own and others' good opinion of me, I proceeded to get almost straight As through college. After Latin from the Hill and Paul High School, English seemed simple, and I had a certain writing skill even then. The initial three month period was spent studying comparative anatomy, dissecting an evil-smelling dogfish that glared balefully at me through the whole process. Still I was not disheartened.

Tony my high-spirited, quarter horse I rode from age fifteen until leaving ranching behind in 1949.

Eldon and Todd with Duke, their collie, on the Lazy Lee Ranch, in 1947.

Dr McAllister taught English. She was a 35 year-old, unmarried PhD who I reckoned was somewhat innocent to the ways of the world. When teaching Chaucer, which has some very raunchy parts indeed, she blushed a scarlet red. The war veterans in her class snickered and were more taken with the reaction of Dr McAllister than they were with the racy tales. Moreover, I judged them less innocent and naive than Dr McAllister; however, Chaucer's story of "The Miller's Tale" *is* pretty spicy.

Chemistry was taught by a cheerful individual, Professor Dietzman. It pleased him to have "the brains" as pupils in his class, and he encouraged stiff competition to bring out the highest possible level of performance.

It was one of his lab sessions, an experiment with raw sodium, that nearly led to my downfall. Sodium in its pure state is extremely volatile, and is preserved in benzene, which is quite flammable. As luck would have it, my French class was right in the middle of the chemistry laboratory time, and in rushing to make French class, I dumped my specimen into the trough that ran along the counter and emptied into a basin at the end.

When I dumped the sodium into the wet trough, it immediately exploded and set the benzene on fire. The whole trough was a mass of flames, and I turned on the taps to extinguish the flames, and in so doing washed the benzene and the sodium down the sink at the end of the trough. This immediately caused another explosion, which blew the grate of the sink to the ceiling, and smoke and fumes filled the lab, necessitating immediate evacuation. At this time I felt it prudent to hasten to my French class. Afterwards I returned to my fate. Professor Dietzman regarded me rather sourly for a moment, then broke into a broad grin and told me to beat it before I destroyed the college.

In French, I carried off the top mark in spite of the fact that I couldn't find my way to the bathroom in the language. However, I knew more French grammar than the professor.

In those days, and probably still, the competition for the places in medical school was fierce. One had to be absolutely committed and completely disciplined to have a hope. Accordingly, I worked extremely hard and achieved high marks. Those who aspired to medical school and did not follow this course either went off to some other discipline or waited for several years to get into medical school.

Seattle Pacific College was a Free Methodist co-ed school, and there was a certain amount of inter-gender communication. The school attempted to regulate this quite strictly, but exceptions occurred. Todd and I had a corner room on the fifth floor of Alexander Hall, a large space walled on one side by a turret. A girls' dorm was immediately behind, and off limits to males. However, it was possible to make paper gliders and write a note on the paper, and with some dexterity, sail it through the open windows of one's favourite female.

In the library, boys and girls sitting next to, or opposite, each other at the reading tables, took off their shoes and rubbed feet under the tables. I suspect this tradition might have been student reaction to a sign that read, "Shoes are to be worn in the library."

I have often wanted to do a scientific study on a phenomenon that I noticed. Since women are

Alexander Hall at Seattle Pacific College under the wind vane is the Lee boys' room.

somewhat reticent on this matter I have not done so, but as an ex-rancher I noticed that some of the girls went into oestrus each month. While many women showed no outward reaction to their fertile time, as a ranch boy I knew that in the animal world females go absolutely bonkers during fertile periods. At any rate, some of the girls appeared to me to go absolutely man crazy for two or three days, presumably at mid-cycle. This may be significant considering that in spite of cows' very obvious oestrus activity, humans number six billion to one billion cows.

A weekend diversion I found extremely pleasant during my Seattle years involved crab hunts at St. Mary's beach 30 miles north of the city. On a good low tide, one waded into the shallows, and with a garden fork reached down into three feet of water and lifted large crabs from the bottom. On one occasion, four of us captured 100 full-sized crabs. We took them back to the college biology department, where there were three-foot stainless steel kettles, and cooked all of them. To everyone, student or professor, we handed a boiled crab and a serviette. The whole college smelled of crabs for a week!

As far as romance was concerned, I had every inclination, but not much time. In addition, the young women in this institution gave signals which were difficult for me to interpret, coming as I did from a different environment. The poet Shelley speaks of this fickleness in a poem, "The light that lies in a woman's eyes, and lies and lies and lies."

At any rate, I was becoming more and more interested in a pretty little Canadian nursing student whom I had met at my aunt's home in Chilliwack. Her name was Marjorie Pearl Cartmell. She was to play a large part in my future life.

On the whole, my first year of pre-med wasn't bad. I was a Summa Cum Laude, which meant I was in the top ten per cent of the freshman class, and I had found my future wife. The following years, however, would yield new adventures.

CHAPTER 5

MEDICAL SCHOOL — GOAL IN SIGHT

The years of pre-med are so intense and so demanding that almost no thought can be given to medical school. The chances of admittance are dicey at best and total concentration is required during pre-med school to gain a level of knowledge requisite for entrance into medical school.

After two years in college, I was confident that I would make the grade and began to apply to medical schools. At this time only about one applicant in ten was accepted, and I was determined to be that one. While some students applied to ten medical schools, I selected three. The first was the University of Washington which was close by, had a good reputation, and would cause the least disruption in my life. The second was the University of Toronto, probably the best medical school in Canada at that time, and the third was the University of British Columbia, whose medical school was newly founded and untried.

Applications to each school involved essentially the same process. First, a request was sent to the school for an application form, together with college transcripts and grades. The next step was to write the medical aptitude test, a

Eldon BSc, Todd BA, 1952 graduates from Seattle Pacific College.

six-hour examination consisting of a thousand general questions. Everything one had learned in a lifetime could come up in this examination. One of the questions on the test was, "On which river does the German city of Hamelin lie?" For me, the answer was simple. It lies on the River Weser. A plotting of a bombing run on this city during my air force days gave me the answer. I suppose "The Pied Piper of Hamelin" by Browning might have been equally helpful.

At any rate, I received replies from all three universities and was much encouraged by an invitation to sit out oral examinations and personal interviews at the University of Washington. My two years in the RCAF was again of help, since veterans were given a preferential position.

Off I trotted the three miles to the University of Washington where my future in medicine was probably decided by two questions. The first was, "What accounts for the degree of density in fatty acids?" and the second, "What World War II General was in charge of NATO?" I answered both correctly and was short-listed to meet a psychiatrist who asked if I had ever been tempted to seduce my mother. Later I apparently gave a suitable answer when the famous Dr Richard Blandau asked me why fertilization ever took place.

After what seemed like an eternity, I received a telephone call from the University of Washington accepting my application for placement in first year medicine. This was in February, and the first class started in September of 1951.

Oh, happy day! I finished up my year, amassing enough points to graduate with a B.Sc., worked all summer in the laboratory at a pulp mill, and proposed to my sweetheart Marjorie, who was at that time a student nurse at the Royal Columbian Hospital in New Westminster, BC.

All in all, it was a most successful year. Medical school awaited and Marjorie and I set a marriage date one year hence when she finished nursing school.

In these halcyon days I was treated with a new respect by my mother and was referred to as, "My son, soon to be the doctor." I was also besieged on all sides to

Eldon, a first-year medical student at the University of Washington.

diagnose aches and pains. A further bonus was that my verdicts were accepted as if they were the opinion of the most prominent specialist.

Whenever possible, relations with colleagues of the future were cultivated. I even remember dropping in for an interview with the head psychiatrist of Riverview Hospital to sound out the prospects of a medical future in psychiatry. He appeared much bemused, but was curious and friendly. I foresaw myself as a colleague of great men such as he, and my self-image as a doctor was gradually heightened and magnified. Little did I realize that nine more years of intensive study were in store for me, and at the conclusion of these years I would still have much to learn in my chosen specialty.

The best attitude when entering medicine is to accept that it is your life for an entire professional career. True, there are many different levels within medicine and the entrance to medical school is at a very humble level indeed, the embarkation point on a continuum to the highest professional status. In the 1950s when I launched my career in medicine I felt ready and willing. What wasn't clear yet, was whether medicine was ready for me.

Oppostie: Crabbing at St. Mary's beach. (Left to right) Brother Todd, girlfriend Thirza Sandborn, friend Dorothy Sandborn, Marjorie and Eldon.

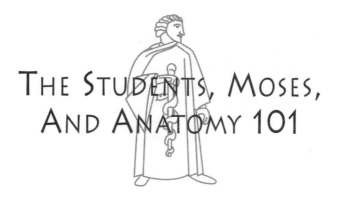

CHAPTER 6

THE STUDENTS, MOSES, AND ANATOMY 101

Prior to the beginning of medical school there was a nagging disquietude among us newcomers. The main cause of this was the realization that we would, for the first time, dissect a human cadaver. Most of us had put in extensive time dissecting frogs, dogfish, and other animals, but the very thought of studying anatomy on a human being, and particularly one which we would dissect, injected an intimidating element of uncertainty.

The start of medical school was abrupt and somewhat traumatic. We, who had stood at the head of our classes in college, were suddenly exposed to seventy-five others who enjoyed a similar position in their studies at different universities.

Almost immediately we started the study of human anatomy. I will never forget the first day. We were led into a large, open room, dominated by rows of steel tables, each with a sheet drawn over a lifeless form. Six students were assigned to each table. There were about sixteen such tables lined up in three rows with about eight feet separating each table. Three of the tables were for special dissections by visiting anatomists.

The professor walked in and said, "All right, begin. Remove the drapes." We removed a green tarp-like sheet to view the subject of our full year's study of anatomy. We found our cadaver to be Negroid, approximately fifty-five years of age who appeared to have had a lot of hard times in his life. His hands were square and thickened with calluses, his muscles were heavily formed, and his frame stocky. Later on we would determine that he had tuberculosis, kidney problems, arthritis, and heart problems. It was also evident that his last meal was of Chinese noodles. I suspected that he was one of the lost souls of the world, destitute and friendless in a big city. I decided he had likely collapsed on the sidewalk on a downtown street. No one had claimed his body. And so it came that his physical remains ended up in the anatomy department of the University of Washington.

At my table was a rather diverse group: two young women, me, a former U.S. fighter jock, and two men younger than me, one a pharmacist, and the other a chap with a master's degree in history.

One of the girls, Nellie, had a fascinating past life. She was from a Jewish family who lived in Vienna, Austria, at the onset of World War II, and by some means was smuggled out through Yugoslavia with her sweetheart. She remembered sitting all night in the railway station in Belgrade in the arms of her companion with bombs exploding all around. In the morning her love stayed behind to join the Underground, and Nellie continued, eventually ending up in Israel. She never heard of her sweetheart again.

In Israel she found that she wasn't much of a prize for marriage. As she explained it, she did not have reading glasses, she still had her appendix, and her teeth were her own, making her somewhat of a risk for matrimony, since any potential husband had to consider these as future expenses. She made her way to Canada, graduated from UBC, and to her delight was accepted at the University of Washington Medical School.

Medical students are a rather irrepressible lot, and by consensus we named our cadaver Moses. Otherwise there was no levity, and we were all conscious that we were dealing with the frame of a fellow human being. To me, his finest gift to society was his body, which would further our knowledge in human anatomy.

We soon found that in spite of white gowns and gloves, our clothing was permeated with the

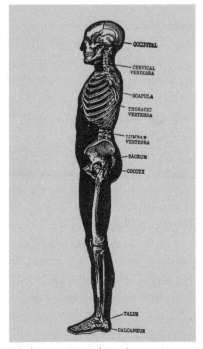

Skeleton print — knee bone connected to the thigh bone. We learned them all.

smell of formaldehyde. It was impossible to eradicate and wherever we went heads turned and nostrils flared at the pungent odour. I suspect that new relationships were slow to form in that first year of medicine!

Our anatomy studies usually started at 8:00 AM and continued until 5:00 PM, one or two days a week. Two people dissected, and one read from the dissecting manual. The other three would kibitz or peruse *Grant's Anatomy Book*. It was a matter of Canadian pride to me that we used the textbook written by C. Boileau Grant of Toronto as our dissecting manual.

Our anatomy professor, Dr Johnson, was demanding and of the same rank as Simon Legree in *Uncle Tom's Cabin*. He was Simon, and we were the slaves. Our dissecting times were often interrupted to accommodate his lectures, which could go on for three hours without a break. He carried a long pointer, and when he saw one of the students nodding off, as would often occur, he would march out among the students, and, without breaking his line of discourse, rap the student on the head with the pointer and then return to the front of the lecture hall. This action brought the whole class to attention. He also had an ability, common to most anatomy professors I have known, of drawing simultaneously with both hands.

Month after month we worked away on our anatomy dissection, memorizing the 206 bones, the hundreds of muscles, the nerves, the arteries, the special organs. Day after day we carried the information from the lectures and our books back to the cadaver and tried to correlate them.

There are at least three systems of naming anatomical structures, and we were expected to remember all three names for each structure. One system was the Birmingham Nomenclature, the second was the Basil Nomina Anatomica of continental Europe and the third, the American Revised. The Basil Nomina Anatomica was somewhat complicated for those who had not had a background in Latin. Thus, for many of us, our memories were tested by the name of the smallest muscles in the body, the *flexor brevis minimi digiti*, which are also known as the flexor of the little finger, or flexor of the fifth digit.

It was inevitable that mnemonics, or memory aids, were used. One which seems to be present in every medical school in the western world goes as follows: "Never lower Tillie's pants; mother might come home." This may seem to be a simple example of the lewd working of a medical student's mind, but the first letter of each word stands for a wrist bone, thus *Navicular, Lunate, Triquetrum, Pisiform, Multiangular Greater, Multiangular Lesser, Capitate,* and *Hamate.*

Another important mnemonic, particularly to surgeons operating on the neck goes as follows: "The lingual nerve took a curve about the hyoglossus. Said Wharton's duct, I'll be mucked, the blighters double-crossed us." There were many more, some of which I have forgotten — obviously not very successful as mnemonics.

Professor Johnson often announced to the class that he was especially interested in a certain nerve or vessel and would request all to be especially careful in dissecting this and to preserve it at all costs. The usual response to this was practically nil, since days before we had completely cut out this particular structure, and it had gone long ago in our cremation bucket.

The second female in our group was Lila. She had the brains of a Ph.D. but the innocence of an eighteen year old farm girl. Deciding that her level of suspicion should be increased for her own good, one day when things were slow, the male members of our team decided it was time to administer the coordination, position, and eye/hand response test. One of the younger members at our table fitted a large funnel with a neck under his belt and then placed a penny on the bridge of his nose. The test was then to flip the penny from his nose into the open funnel. After this had been demonstrated a few times, it was suggested that Lila take this important test to prove she had the coordination to make a proper doctor.

I watched as Nellie, who was used to the ways of students, frowned in disapproval, but she said nothing, and Lila blithely proceeded with the test. The neck of the funnel was placed inside the front of her skirt, and the penny put on the bridge of her nose in the approved fashion. Of course, before she could flip the penny into the funnel, someone came from behind and poured a litre of ice water into the funnel. Lila shrieked, and the professor grew red-faced and very angry. Amid laughter we rationalized that heightening her awareness helped her to avoid many similar scams in the future.

The lectures were given in an amphitheatre with a central stage and rows of seats in a circle, at increasing elevations. Once, when a visiting dignitary was invited to give a lecture, all the students in the front row had a letter written in white chalk on the sole of their shoe. On cue they raised their right foot onto the railing, and the letters read "Welcome to UW, Professor Smith."

One of our lecturers was the famous Dr Von Neurath, the world authority on protein chemistry. Since he had a strong German accent, and his subject was very complex, I could hardly make head or tail of anything that he taught. After forty years the one thing I did remember was this fragment of a German poem given in one of his lectures:

Mein lieber Freund und Student wohl
Der grosse Feind ist Alkohol.
Aber es ist in der Bibel geschrieben
Sie muessen die Feinde lieben.

My dear friend and student
Your great enemy is alcohol.
But it is written in the Bible
That you must love your enemy.

Some of the greatest traumas in the first year of Anatomy 101 were the practical tests. These were unannounced, and the only warning would be when at eight o'clock we arrived outside the dissecting room to find that the doors were locked. Professor Johnson, who sometimes worked all night to set up the tests, would open the doors, and each student would start at a table. On each cadaver would be a little numbered sticker, and one was required to correctly name the designated anatomical structure. If the little flag was on a structure on the right side of the body, one had to note that it was a right-sided structure. If this was not noted, two points were taken off, for as the professor said, if you take out a right-sided structure when you should take out the left, it may well lead to disaster.

During the year we came to marvel at the human body. Over 200 bones make up the bony frame. To these are attached hundreds of muscles and ligaments. Each knee had eleven ligaments to govern its movement and position. It is no wonder that professional athletes damage this finely-tuned structure, and it explains why the great hockey player, Bobby Orr, will forever have stiff knees. In June came the final dissection class, fittingly enough on the foot. The six of us bade our final farewell to Moses and all passed Anatomy 101.

What of those who attended at Table #6, the amiable group of students and professors who, for a year, had abided with Moses?

Professor Johnson went on to academic fame with textbooks bearing his name and professorships in famous universities. Professor Von Neurath lives to this day, and in 1995 I heard that at the ripe old age of eighty-seven he received an honorary Ph.D. in Japan. He had a rich and fulfilling life with many honours gained.

Of the six medical students, two became general practitioners, one rich and successful, the second unhappy and a failure. Two became specialists, one a neurologist, and myself a gynecologist. Lila of the bubbly, innocent personality, gained her doctorate, married, had children, and lived happily ever after.

It was to Nellie Gutman Auersperg that the greatest honours came. She received her M.D., then a Ph.D., and went on to write many scientific papers. She did a great deal of useful work on human cell cultures and in the field of cancer cell behaviour. She is now full Professor at the University of British Columbia.

What of Moses? Shakespeare says that the evil that men do lives after them, but the good is often interred with their bones. With Moses, the evil of his past was likely interred before his bones. As a result of those bones, good lives on in the knowledge and skill of the doctors that studied so hard in Anatomy 101. Let no one say that Moses was mean or base or without value. His body was an instrument by which good came to this world, and knowledge to benefit the human race was advanced. Let this be a paean to time everlasting: rest in peace, Moses.

CHAPTER 7

COUNTY HOSPITAL

After three years of pre-medicine at our respective colleges and universities and two years of hard academics in medical school, we were assigned to King County Hospital, also called th Harborview Hospital, to spend a further two years immersed in clinical hospital work. Harborview Hospital was a monstrous grey stone building set on a rise overlooking downtown Seattle and Elliott Bay.

The United States of America has an institution which has no counterpart in Canada: the County Hospital or Charity Hospital. Many private hospitals exist for those who can afford them but the charity hospital is for the gross, the lame, the dispossessed, the burned out, the psychotic, the derelict, the alcoholic, and the stricken poor. It is also a refuge for the middle class whose illness has outlasted their financial ability. No one is ever turned away from the County Hospital, and here medical care begins and ends for the poor.

I was first introduced to clinical medicine at Harborview Hospital. The hospital had 750 beds and smelled of disinfectant, age-old urine, and poverty. At that time it was almost ninety years old.

Our class was welcomed to the hospital by the medical director who was built somewhat like Boss Hogg, the cartoon oinker of television fame, complete with a fat cigar. Ignoring gender, he addressed us collectively as "boys" (a generalization far more acceptable in those days) and told us we would be getting our introduction to medicine as he had many years before. He said he would teach us a few things which, in our strictly scientific approach, had been neglected. That was the art and practice of medicine.

Fresh from learning the latest classroom knowledge, we looked at him askance. I'm sure we were all thinking that this derelict from a dinosaur park could teach us very little. In fact he taught us, in an hour's time, a great deal about people and medicine that the nearby university had ignored.

"Listen to what the patient tells you," he said, "and observe him as a person. The patient will show you or tell you his problem, and what you need to do is watch and listen."

He asked an orderly to bring down a few patients, and asked each individual a few questions, thanked them, and then excused them.

"Watch how they walk," he told us. "Do they stand straight, are they beaten and slumped, do they shuffle, do they look you in the eye, do they smile, or do they look glum or completely broken? Look at the patient clinically. Are they swollen, are they pink, yellow, white, or blue? Do they limp, are they emaciated? Are they feeling the floor with their feet, or do they lack sensation in their lower limbs?"

At the end of his session, we were wiser. I still remember that first hour he spent with us.

In our first few months at the hospital, we found need for all his wisdom. The medical wards in the County Hospital had twenty-six beds, ten placed vertically to each side wall, and six down the centre. Every slum, every flop house, every old people's hospital, and every gutter in Seattle had its representative on our ward.

They came to die. Very few were ever released from this ward. Each was a walking museum of pathology. In twenty-six days we lost twenty-eight patients. Despite our best efforts, the patients died like flies. In short order, it became impossible to be compassionate. When patients die at such a rate, emotional involvement with them would destroy one's mental stability. Still, we tried to administer a reasonable standard of medicine, and each of us worked sixteen hours a day, seven days a week, in this endeavour.

A case in point was a patient who was brought in one evening in very poor condition. He was blue, short of breath, and his heart raced. An electrocardiogram, running continuously, showed wild fluctuations. The senior house doctor was called. He examined the patient, studied the electrocardiogram, and found in the old man's pockets a bottle of digitalis pills, a heart medicine. Some pills were missing, and the question was whether the old man needed to take the medicine or had already had too much. The senior house doctor's name was McCarthy, and I can still picture him. He decided that the patient had not had enough medicine, rather than too much. He

gave an injection intravenously of a digitalis preparation. The old man stiffened, grew bluer, stopped breathing, had a cardiac arrest, and died.

We all stood still, and were stunned. McCarthy took one look at the patient and said, "I think he had too much," and turned on his heel and walked away. One by one we returned to other necessary tasks, still unable to comprehend the significance of the event. Only the events of living connected us to reality again and kept us mentally balanced.

At King County, patients held their meager possessions against their chests. Items often disappeared during the course of the patient's illness in spite of this, causing dismay. Other days a display of compassion lit up the ward. One day an old black man lay in his bed, his few possessions cradled against his chest. The man next to him craved a smoke. The old Negro held out two cigars, probably his last, and all he could hope to see in the future. He looked at the smokeless gentleman and said, "Here, have one of my cigars." This simple act brightened the ward, and, for a time at least, the staff went about their duties with a sense of cheerfulness and warmth that had not been there earlier in the shift.

The maternity ward was always busy, as poor people could not afford maternity care outside of County Hospital. There were endless obstetrical complications to address. In those days, with a Caesarean-section rate of less than three percent, women had long, hard labours and often forceps were used with very little relief from pain. Still there were humourous times, as the day when an older black lady with her tenth child laboured valiantly on. The staff were distracted, as the tugboat race on Elliott Bay could be easily seen through the window. The house staff would rush to the window to watch the tugboats steaming across the bay, and then with the next groan from the nearby bed, turn their attention to the lady again. Was it a coincidence that she named the baby Steamboat Jackson?

One day the obstetrical houseman and the junior housemen were having coffee in Harborview's basement cafeteria. An emergency call came from the maternity ward, and as luck would have it, none of the elevators were functioning. There was no alternative but to run the nine floors up to the maternity ward. When the junior

A Seattle landmark institution, King County Hospital, also known as Harborview Medical Center, has its main entrance on 9th Street.

houseman reached the ward, the more senior houseman, plump and out of shape, lagged two floors behind. They found the head nurse running down the hallway with a tiny, premature baby, who was quite blue. The mother, a scrawny, 15-year old, had hastened the delivery of this premature baby while in the nurse's care. The nurse rushed him to the nursery as the doctors just arrived. This crisis was resolved but one wondered what future lay before this new mother and baby.

There is an anonymous saying, "If the saddest words of tongue and pen are those, 'It might have been', sadder these we daily see, 'It is but hadn't ought to be.'"

The women's ward, or gynecology ward, had a curious mix of patients. There were people with terminal cancer, and street girls, most often admitted with pelvic infections.

One woman lives on in my memory still. Her story was common enough. In spite of warning signs of cancer, her husband, a dominating and overbearing type, would not let her seek medical attention. When she finally arrived at Harborview Hospital, she had far-advanced cancer. She was emaciated, racked with pain, and filled with misery. One could see that she both loathed her husband and hated her body which was destroying her. There was no hope, no joy, only the misery of a slow progression to death.

The wasting of the disease had left her with very blue eyes, which were set off by the whiteness of her skin. Looking at her I was struck by the unusual beauty of her eyes and remarked with complete sincerity and spontaneity that she had the "loveliest blue eyes." For a brief moment she smiled and said, "Do you really think so?" There could be no doubt as to the sincerity of my observation, but I still marvel at how the mind clings to a body that is hopelessly lost. She went on to her inevitable end a few days later.

The women's ward offered its own brand of levity. Rodney, one of the housemen, was a case in point. How Rodney ever got into medicine was a mystery. He was so painfully shy that he blushed whenever a woman came into the room. He could not even take a woman's blood pressure without becoming red and perspiring. Rodney was actually a nice-looking boy, about 5'10", with straight black hair, a broad mouth, and brown eyes with a few twinkle marks, but he absolutely panicked at the sight of a woman. The street girls would tease him and say, "Rodney, it's about time for my annual check-up, don't you think?" Or, "If you get sleepy in the afternoon, dearie, remember where you can lay your head for a nap." At this, Rodney would turn ten shades of scarlet and slink away in abject mortification.

During our stay on the women's ward, each one of us had to make an extensive evaluation and examination of a female patient and present this to the professor. Rodney knew two things: one, that there was no escape from this presentation, and two, that there was no way in the world that he would be able to examine a woman and present her case in detail.

Finally, he did the only thing open to him. He "dry labbed" it; that is, he reviewed all the notes and the examination findings of every other doctor who had treated his patient, and when his presentation day came, he stood up to present his test case.

The house staff stood in a circle nudging each other, expecting Rodney's usual shyness to take over. The professor somewhat absentmindedly reminded him to get started, and Rodney, much to our surprise, spoke up clearly and in great detail, and described every mark and scar and finding, both out and inward. The professor nodded, visibly impressed, and all the housemen were dumbfounded, wondering if Rodney had responded to one of the street girls' invitations, and in some mysterious fashion been emancipated from his bashfulness.

The patient, earthy, candid and a tartish constrast to Rodney, looked on in amazement. Finally able to stand it no longer, she blurted out, "What's with this guy? He knows more about me than my old man, and I've never seen him before in my life!" Poor Rodney. Women continued to be a problem through his medical life and later his marriage failed.

Life was played out in the streets of Seattle, but the final curtain usually fell in the County Hospital. So it was one evening when the police happened upon a major bank robbery in North Seattle after an alarm had sounded. The police arrived just as the robbers were leaving the bank. As pistol shots scattered, six police covered the front of the bank. Instead of bringing the robbers to ground with their shotguns, the battle developed into one of hand guns. The problem was that the robbers were dead shots, and before the action ended, four policemen were on the ground, and the robbers escaped in a stolen car.

The policemen were brought into King County Hospital in the evening, two directly to the morgue, and two to the surgical floor. All had been shot in the upper abdomen. After many hours of surgery, the two were still alive, but in critical condition, and indeed did survive after many operations and months in hospital. This event dramatically brought home to us the hazards of police work.

There was an international flavour to this event, as one of the robbers' pistols was dug up months later in Stanley Park in Vancouver, BC, apparently on an insider's tip. To my knowledge, the murderers were never apprehended.

The children's ward in Harborview Hospital was filled with the offspring of the poor, the deprived, and the underprivileged. It was always a joy to see young children, sweet and innocent, but the most heart-rending events in medicine also occurred on the children's ward.

I recall one fifteen-year old girl, who should have been attending high school and prom parties. She had a kind of nasty malignant tumour that occasionally befalls teenagers, known as Ewing's sarcoma. Having failed to respond to radiation, she was admitted to hospital for high amputation of her thigh. It was hard to accept that this lovely young woman, who should have been running and dancing and walking, would be from that time on lurching and crippled with an artificial limb.

It was a very emotional scene the night before, and at about ten o'clock that night she still had not signed her consent. She said, "If I could just walk around the block, I think I could face this operation tomorrow."

Harborview Hospital is located on one of the meanest streets in North America, and at ten o'clock at night there was serious risk involved in such an outing. In fact, people have been mugged outside of King County Hospital in broad daylight.

Dr Eldon Lee would deliver over 4,500 babies during his active career.

Finally, the nurse and houseman summoned the biggest and toughest looking orderly in the hospital. Together with the young girl they made their way out of the hospital and along the sidewalks of two square blocks. The girl walked along, feeling the sidewalk with both feet, then went into the gutter to feel that, then up on small portions of lawn which bordered the sidewalk, and finally up the steps, two at a time, into the hospital lobby. When they arrived back at the ward she said, "I can face it now," and signed her consent. The next morning she went for the amputation.

One of the most pathetic images I still recall occurred the day that nurses wheeled three little urchins into the isolation portion of the ward. They had been apprehended by the social workers as children in need of care, either deserted or abused by their parents. They came to us, parentless, covered in measles, burning with fever, and coughing the harsh bark of bronchitis, all grouped in a single bed. They had no clothes on; these probably had been dispatched to the incinerator. The children sat up with a single blanket drawn around them. They clung to each other, all the misery and fear and dismay of the world showing in their eight-, six-, and four-year old bodies. The only thing they had in the world was each other; everything else had failed them.

Those looking after them felt the misery of their plight, and the sight still haunts me. I can only hope that in their later life they continued to draw strength from each other's company as they did on that hospital day.

The doctors and nurses I knew drew strength from their commitment to each other and the many very ill patients, in spite of the inadequate facilities and the fact that they were very few and overworked. They showed more humanity and compassion than they were given credit for; perhaps even more than the cheerful, rested doctors and nurses shown in this present day.

CHAPTER 8

Love And Marriage In The World Of Medicine

The most difficult decision a male doctor must make is his choice of a mate. It takes a combination of angel, saint, and chief executive officer with a master's degree to fill the position of a doctor's wife. To meet the challenge she must be loving and supportive, calm in times of stress, resolute in times of decision making, and completely unflappable in times of utter chaos.

She must have the qualities of Saint Theresa combined with the firmness of Margaret Thatcher. Somehow she must be chef, nurturing enchantress, brownie pack leader, and head of numerous charitable committees and church causes — all this to stand by a husband whose duties take him away at all times of day and night, and whose ordinary work schedule may demand twelve to sixteen hours per day. She must cope with a doctor-husband arriving home at nine o'clock, emotionally and physically drained. The superb meal she planned for seven o'clock is now dry, overdone, and tasteless. The wife may likewise be burned up. Man and wife must, together, overcome.

The utter irregularity of a doctor's life can be a constant source of frustration, both to the doctor and his wife, but the rules of commitment to medicine demand a steadfast and ongoing obligation to patients in need at any time of the day or year.

One profound bit of advice given to a group of doctors' wives by a woman who left their ranks was to the effect that a woman should never marry a doctor. "You never see him, and you're always pregnant." The woman who gave this advice was single again, with two children. It is a tough job, not meant for everybody. The failure rate is daunting. Fifty percent of medical students who marry during their years of university will eventually divorce.

There are sinister forces for medical men to contend with. A doctor's role in a community is usually respected and admired, and some girls find it difficult to keep their hands off. Possibly the doctor's position is analogous to that of a Catholic priest. His sexual integrity may be a challenge to some adventurous young women intent on taking him to bed. This does nothing for the young woman's reputation, but it destroys the reputation of the young professional. Stresses beset and try every marriage, but are more pronounced for a doctor and spouse. The rate of failure of both romances and marriages remain high in comparison to many other professions.

One advantage that a doctor's family normally possesses is that, with time, financial worries decrease. However, too much money can also be a problem. A dose of money is no replacement when meaningful contact is minimized by the constraint of time. A slick car may be offered as a balancing chip. Instead of allotting time so leisurely camping trips can cement the relationship between children and parents, busy doctors, with the means to do so, send children to Disneyland with friends or their solo wife filling dual parental roles.

There is, in addition, an insidious force that inflicts and divides doctors and their wives. This consists of the changes to an individual's very makeup. The idealistic, enthusiastic, lovable student in second year university marrying the shy, pretty, young female student, nurse or secretary may not bear much likeness to the doctor who graduates after an intensive struggle of eight or twelve years. The two who promised to remain steadfast, faithful, and loving, until death do them part, find that time changes all.

Nothing is more saddening or common than the situation where a wife, who has worked through the years to put the husband through medical school and seen him establish a successful practice, finds herself cast aside for someone deemed more suitable for soul development in his new role.

Casualties of modern medicine? One of my fellow students at U of W got his chance to go to medical school only because his wife worked steadily as a secretary for five years. He responded by handing her a divorce writ on graduation day, and took off with a nubile temptress who more fittingly filled the wife model he had in mind at that time. Fortunately the courts are showing less patience with this scenario.

Husband, wife, and children alike must learn to respect the maintenance of family structure as their first priority. The family is the basic unit for any social grouping and can only be kept strong and rich by constant devotion, loyalty, and attention. No realist can ever accept this to be an easy task.

Having said that, there are other relevant factors such as luck, willingness to take chances in a human relationship, and a certain amount of cheering from friends and family, that can help marriages survive.

When we met, Marjorie and I were both ready to establish a serious relationship with someone. In the backs of our minds, we were each quietly sizing up potential mates. Even so, we did not get off to an auspicious start. My aunt Madeline had schemed to bring the two of us together.

It began one foggy night in Marjorie's home town of Chilliwack, BC. She was paddling along a secondary road. I was driving the same route on this misty, dark evening of early fall. Suddenly a bicycle and a female form appeared ahead of me on the edge of the street. Only by hastily veering the car was I able to swing around without hitting her. I apologized through the foggy space between the car and the bicycle and continued on to my aunt's nearby home. I was much surprised when a few minutes later the same cyclist came through the door, fixing me with a less than appreciative gaze. The fact that Marjorie did not stomp out in annoyance was an indication that she possessed the qualities of forgiveness and tolerance which were to become valuable assets as our relationship progressed. Indeed, during the evening we established some communication, and found a mutual compatibility. We occasionally met at family functions and church doings and at these social events tended to pair off more and more. We shared events with friends, as a couple, and soon we were inclined to spend two or three hours or more in embraces, parked on the levy by the lazy Fraser River. Big band music of Glenn Miller or Tommy and Jimmy Dorsey came from our car radio and provided a dreamy, romantic atmosphere to discuss serious matters and cuddle just a little bit longer.

It caused some consternation in Marjorie's family when I brought her home at one or two o'clock in the morning. I was reminded by my aunt that a respectable hour would be more consistent with the conduct of a Salvation Army officer's daughter, which Marjorie was.

The intense concentration required in my own studies and the 120-miles between the University of Washington and Marjorie's nursing school restricted courtship. The distance between us seemed too long.

In my first year of medicine, plans were made for marriage without serious thought given to dates, although it was understood that our marriage date was to be planned after Marjorie's graduation from Royal Columbian Nursing School in New Westminster. At the end of my first year and six weeks prior to Marjorie's graduation she informed me that her father was to be out west soon, and wondered if that would be a convenient time to be married. I hadn't seriously considered a wedding date, so busy was I in my studies, but it seemed like a proposal that I couldn't turn down, and so it was arranged.

Wedding bells, 22 August 1952, Chilliwack, BC.

I entered into marriage with the sure knowledge that Marjorie was not a great cook, a matter which had not gone unnoticed by my mother. For me this was offset by her outgoing personality and her strong nurturing abilities developed from her family's commitment to the Salvation Army. She also played the tenor horn in the Salvation Army Band, a dubious asset.

On an August weekend in 1952, before 150 relatives and friends, we were duly married by Marjorie's father, Brigadier Cartmell. After a big reception in St. Peter's Anglican Hall in Chilliwack, we cut the cake prepared by Marjorie's aunt Bessie and were sent off on a three-day honeymoon.

Like the proper couple in Rupert Brooks's poem, "Sonnet Reversed" where: *Still he went Cityward daily; still she did abide at home. And both were really quite content with work and social pleasures.* Life assumed a tranquil pace for both of us. We returned to Seattle where Marjorie gained employment at Firland's TB Sanatorium. Daily I went forth to university, and daily Marjorie went to her nursing chores. I had invested the fruits of my ranching career in a two-bedroom house in Seattle, bought for $800 down. Total payments were $42 a month, and expenses minimal. The $500 tuition to be paid to the University of Washington was saved during my work as a summer student.

We were happy in our new home; I enjoyed my studies and financially we were secure. But time does not stand still. Marjorie was like most young brides, who on seeing a newborn baby get that mystic look in their eyes, and without

Eldon Lee, MD, Marjorie Lee RN. Love and Marriage.

being a mental genius in family dynamics, I realized a child would soon be part of our life. In addition, in 1955 I graduated from medicine and this required a move to continue my postgraduate studies. Our Seattle home sold readily to a newly wedded couple for a $200 profit. Marjorie's Uncle Harold loaned us his truck, and with the small expense of gas and the help of a cousin or two we moved ourselves from Seattle to Vancouver, BC.

There I earned the princely sum of $25 a month as an intern, and since our apartment cost $90 a month in rent, there was a negative balance which for a time threatened our financial position. Marjorie, although pregnant with our first child, supplemented our income with specialty nursing. Monthly I contributed my $25 salary to the common weal, and somehow we survived.

The essence of married life is survival. I am sure it was helped by Marjorie's upbringing where she learned to skimp a bit where necessary. She had learned the qualities of nurturing, tenderness, caring, and always put as a first priority our home and family. In addition, religion, background and family ties strengthened our position. Always we realized that this little ship was ours, and whether it floated or sank depended on our love, our energy, our wisdom and solidarity.

Each year we gave thanks for surviving the previous year and expressed our fervent wish that we could successfully make the coming year a better one.

CHAPTER 9

THE YOUNG INTERN OF VANCOUVER GENERAL HOSPITAL

That interval between graduation from medical school and the beginning of internship is a high point of anyone's early medical life. This is a time when dreams have become a reality, yet the reality is not attended with responsibilities. It is a time when one becomes a colleague of all the current medical men and an heir to the traditions of all great men in medicine from ages past. It is a time when one claims for himself the appellation "Doctor," and one's mother begins all introductions to her friends as "My son, the doctor." Unfortunately these halcyon days end all too soon, and the ending is precipitous, calamitous, and devastating. From the lofty heights one is cast abruptly into the lowly state of an intern.

My arrival at Vancouver General Hospital was a week tardy, courtesy of the late graduation time from American universities. When I arrived I was greeted with both great enthusiasm and exhaustion by my co-worker on the orthopaedic ward, Dr Walt McDonald. Due to my late arrival, he had been working around the clock for a full week. After his heartfelt greeting, he said, "Goodbye," and "I'll see you," and went straight to bed. I busied myself drawing four white uniforms from the storeroom and arrived to do my first day on the ward. Later I found that Walter and I were to room together for a year, which was a serendipitous happening, since he was a cheerful bloke and always did at least his share of all work.

The Vancouver Hospital did not spoil its house staff with telephones in their rooms, but there was a buzzer which the switchboard operator would ring. We would then go out into the hallway to pick up the house phone and were connected to the ward that required our services.

One night I heard Walt's buzzer go, and saw him head towards the phone in his pyjamas. When he didn't return a half hour later, I rose to see what had happened. I found him fast asleep in the telephone cubicle, the telephone on his lap, and feeble buzzes going unheeded.

The whole internship year was so busy and clouded with mind-numbing, sleepless nights, that it seems mostly a blur. However, certain incidents have been retained in my memory. The first of these followed a call to the medical ward at 1:00 AM I arrived to find an elderly patient bleeding heavily from an open wound in his abdomen. There is no event more dramatic than the sight of fresh blood on white sheets at this time of the morning. I started an intravenous, poured in fluid, and started blood running on a pump. In the true spirit of of the famous Canadian Doctor Osler, I called the next of kin, comforted the stricken patient, and called the attending physician. He was satisfied that the situation was reasonably under control, but the family was anxious, and I called him back again and told him that the family would be much comforted if he would attend in person.

The physician was Dr King, an elderly family doctor, who lived in nearby Shaughnessy, and in about forty minutes he arrived, and to my surprise I found him clean shaven and dressed formally in a suit and tie. He took the situation in, and while he could see that his patient was stricken, he concluded that the situation was under control. Dr King thanked me and spoke with the family.

I learned something from this. The next day he came to thank me and gave a bit of background in regard to his patient's condition. The man was terminally ill with cancer, and no matter what was done, he was doomed. My rapid, massive infusions had staved off death for a day or two only. I was impressed at the importance of the art in medicine, as opposed to a strictly scientific approach. Dr King's kind and professional manner made a profound impression upon me.

These were times when there was a more formal relationship between the attending staff and the house staff than exists in modern times. The attending staff were the consultants in the varying specialties and the house staff were the interns, resident doctors and also the nursing staff.

It was my good fortune to know some of the grand old men in medicine in British Columbia who set a fine example for my generation in matters relating to patient care and in disciplines they applied to their own lives. One stern taskmaster was Dr Alan Mackenzie, a senior attending man of Vancouver General's surgery department. He once asked me what interns earned, and I said we were paid twenty-five dollars a month. To this he replied that he had never yet known an intern who was worth that much. From Al Mackenzie we would accept this without resentment, for we knew he would not expect us to experience any hardships that he himself had not experienced.

I once had had a terrible night, being up continuously with several very sick people on the ward. I was slated to assist Dr Mackenzie with surgery at 8:00 AM but at 7:45 I made a quick trip to the residence to shave and put on a clean outfit. I attended Dr Mackenzie a few minutes late. There was no way out of it. I knew I would get it, and Dr Mackenzie gave me the full blast. With him there were no excuses. One stood at attention and said "Yes sir," then, after his dressing down, took one's place as assistant.

In medicine I have often cared for unfortunate people who have experienced a stroke. One poor woman on our ward was left speechless and with some paralysis, although she had all of her mental powers. She was not able to walk and would not eat. In those days, when patient's rights were not paramount, she was forcibly fed with a feeding tube.

It fell my lot to insert the tube for a number of days, and she grew to hate me and fought as much as she could. The look of antipathy in her eyes and her actions were such that I grew to hate myself. But in those days, if a feeding tube was ordered, a feeding tube was inserted and gastric feedings were instituted.

An episode which showed the futility of medical care concerned an elderly professional gentleman who, while not old in years, was likely suffering from Alzheimer's. He had absolutely no memory left and made no sensible speech. Outwardly he looked to be a healthy sixty-year old, but there was no turning of his mental wheels. He tended to lie back in his bed, motionless, and bedsores were almost inevitable. I emphasized to the nurses the importance of getting him up and moving, and insisted this be done frequently. He was fed through a nasal tube to bring up his nutrition. The nurses responded to my enthusiasm and entered into his treatment program with a good deal of spirit. But unfortunately, at the end of intensive efforts we still had a person with no quality of life. One had to wonder if indeed this was a useful effort.

One of the few times where my care as an intern made a difference was a night when a two-year old baby was brought in with croup and respiratory distress. He was put into a steam tent, and I was to sit and watch him. This I did all night long and counted his respirations and checked his colour. At about five o'clock the following morning I could see that his colour was going and that his respirations were becoming more rapid and laboured. I got everyone up and even alerted an ear, nose and throat surgeon. The baby was taken immediately for an emergency tracheotomy and came back an hour later, with good colour and easier respirations, and survived. This baby might well have gotten away on us if he had not been constantly observed.

Some of the in-service clinics provided unusual or bizarre experiences for the interns. The infertility day in the gynaecology clinic yielded one of these unusual experiences. The situation which piqued our interest concerned a young man who brought his two girlfriends into the gynaecology clinic. One was a curvy blonde, while the other was a rather stringy, homely girl, considerably older than he. The Don Juan brashly announced that he would marry the first one who got pregnant. This promise was solemnly noted by all, including Mrs Hudson, our head nurse, who to our amusement, insisted on a level playing field; that is, the lad so anxious to sow his seed was not to spend six nights with his luscious blonde and one night with his older woman. Each was to receive equal attention from the self-deemed progenitor. As luck would have it, it was the

The young interns of Vancouver General Hospital, 1956. The author is standing above the cup; Walt McDonald is seated second from the right.

homely girl who conceived, and when this was confirmed at the clinic, she glowed and gloated. The young man would have happily reneged on his promise, except Mrs Hudson reminded him that she expected a fair conclusion to the whole proceedings. The younger blonde, fed up with her rival, stormed out in a rage. I am not sure what the outcome was, but we knew we had tried to make sure that fair play reigned on this bizarre stage of human drama.

Books and films have been written about the sex life of interns, but my experience suggests they were highly exaggerated, as everyone was constantly exhausted. At Vancouver General, there were two standing house rules. One was that interns were not allowed in the student nurses' residences, and the other that student nurses were at all times off limits. This may have been because the registered nurses wanted to keep any eligible interns as their own preserve. The student nurses were called "Mrs King's Little Virgins," and every effort was made by the senior nursing staff to ensure that this state prevailed.

Young brides who had married graduating doctors in the interval before internship, expecting a glowing year of young passion, were sadly disappointed. After spending a night in the hospital, most interns were so exhausted the following evening when they went home to candles and wine that they fell asleep shortly after leaving the table, only to wake up the next morning at six o'clock to go back to the hospital.

The usual activity for unmarried doctors was exemplified by Bergen, who, having a Saturday off every two weeks, looked forward to getting laid and getting drunk as a means to dispel tensions. Since there were always a few nurses with the same agenda, Bergen was able to connect without any difficulty, but seemed to have a very morose attitude toward the whole business.

During my year as an intern I was propositioned twice by females. One I thought not a very ego-lifting experience when a rather homely forty-year old handed me a note. On it was written, "Dear brown eyes, my husband will be away a week Thursday. Come at three o'clock. P.S. Be sure you're well rested." I walked out of the room, tore the note up, and put it in the garbage.

The second situation was a little more complex. One of the ward nurses confided that her husband was a fat slob who sat and drank beer and watched the television all day, and there was no hope for her to ever get pregnant by him. She desperately wanted a baby.

She said, "Your wife is pregnant; surely she doesn't need you all the time. Couldn't I just borrow you for one or two days a month?"

I had to tell her that my wife was not that broad-minded. Some time later, I noticed that her figure developed noticeably, and I wondered if my friend Dr Bergen had solved her problem.

One of the events which created a good deal of levity was when the administration held Dr McCarthy, a budding specialist in training, up on the charge that he had bedded a young woman overnight in the doctors' residence. His reply was, "Yes, I had a young woman up to my room overnight. Would you prefer I had a young fellow?" This broke up the inquiry.

The last day of my internship was marred by an event which taught me a lesson. As I was about to leave the ward an elderly gentleman had a cardiac arrest and died. I felt it was my responsibility to notify the family and I telephoned his residence. His wife answered, and I told her that her husband had passed away suddenly. She gave a piercing scream, and I could hear the telephone drop and hit the floor, while she sobbed in the background. From this I learned that one should never break news like this over the telephone. Someone should always go in person to speak to the next of kin.

The last evening of internship was a near riot. All the frustrations and anger stored up from a year of hardship and overwork and sleeplessness boiled to the surface. Beer flowed, and after a time the fire hoses were unleashed. Water ran down the steps of the doctors' residence like Niagara Falls in flood. Someone also stuck a fire hose outside the window from the third floor and filled a convertible parked outside the front entrance with water.

One of the interns, Dr Don Stringer, who was to be married the next day, was put into a full body cast in the upstairs bathtub by his inebriated colleagues and unceremoniously dumped in front of the hospital emergency. There one of the pediatric residents, Dr Mogadam, cut the cast off, and noted that Dr Stringer had no clothes on. In this state, Stringer streaked from the emergency department a block and a half to the doctors' residence.

At the conclusion of all this activity the interns surfaced the next day to claim their certificates in a hung over and sorry state. To their great annoyance, the certificates of about twelve who were judged by the administrators to be ringleaders were withheld. Since it was impossible to go into postgraduate work or practise without a certificate, much consternation was felt, and our attending men assembled an appeal board to deal with this situation.

The administration presented their case and looked to the senior medical men to bring down a suitable punishment on the disdained dozen. One elderly doctor looked at a fellow and said, "These modern interns certainly are a dull bunch; hardly any life in them at all. I remember when we were interns we had a still in the basement, and a month before every party all the alcohol on the wards would disappear."

The others answered, "Yes, and remember Dr So-and-so, who used to get up on top of the doctors' residence at three o'clock in the morning and blow a bugle. Why, one night alone the police came out three times and just about closed the residence down."

Faced with this candor, the administration glumly relented and gave everyone their certificates.

The next day we all bade goodbye to the house fathers who looked after our residence through the year. They were amiable, seasoned individuals who had listened to our complaints, encouraged us, and

Marjorie with Gerald Edward. Still to come: Victoria, Barbara, Peter, Robert, and Stuart.

provided guidance when necessary. Out of our meagre monthly stipend we amassed a collection of one hundred dollars for each one of them.

One final event left a lasting impression on me. The girls from the telephone switchboard were invited to a farewell tea by the interns. There were eight to ten of them who through the year had been pleasant, sometimes firm, or persuasive, but always gentle and friendly. They came, and we who had known them only from their voices were taken aback. These were girls who were hired for their voices, and almost all of them had major physical problems. Some were paralyzed, some were in braces and hunchbacked, some had legs shortened and crippled from polio, and some had major spinal deformities. Through the year, influenced solely by their voices, we had no idea they carried such a physical load. I like to think that had we known this, we would not have been so sharp with them when, spent and sleepy, we were called to the phone.

Truly, the experiences as an intern prepared us for the life in medicine that was to follow. Nothing could be harder work, so fraught with stress and sleeplessness. We had stood the time of testing. We were ready for the next year. For some it was as medical officer in the war of Korea, for others general practice in small communities, but for Marjorie and me, it was more of the same; my first year of training as a surgical specialist.

CHAPTER 10

JAMES FLYNN, MISS CHAPMAN, AND THE ELECT

During my year of internship some events stand out starkly in my memory perhaps because they illustrate the frailty and fallibility of people. In a doctor's medical practice such human traits are encountered every day. A fifty-year old derelict, a proper, starched head nurse, a devoted nun, and myself, a hard-working young intern, were the characters involved in this following tale.

Indeed, the story is, well, somewhat unusual, mainly because the characters involved are unusual and the heavenly divinations inscrutable to the minds of personkind.

My first introduction to James Flynn came at 10:00 PM in 1956, on a rainy night in the emergency department of Vancouver General Hospital, approached off Heather Street. It was a slightly run-down emergency department, but it had operated since 1880 and dealt with every sort of emergency occurring in the middle of a great city. It is my belief that one of its greatest trials presented itself in the 5'7", ill-conditioned frame of one James Flynn, one of the poor of the world, supposed to be blessed, but in fact not singularly blessed.

It was not that he smelled or that he was dirty or that he reeked of cheap wine, although he possessed all of these social liabilities; no, it was his regular habit of presenting himself precisely at ten o'clock, shambling in and collapsing on the nearest stretcher from which he proceeded to snore stertorously, puffy, bewhiskered cheeks blowing in and out like bellows, making sounds halfway between a foghorn and a distressed cow. It was impossible to remove him from our emergency department until the morning came.

I was assigned to emergency for three months, and every third night, as regular as a clock, James Flynn would stumble through the door at ten o'clock, and we would care for him over the night, making sure that he had a reasonable breakfast before discharging him into the interminable Vancouver rain.

Since James had most of the major medical conditions described in great medical tomes, it was not difficult to justify keeping him in emergency. All that was required was that one choose the medical condition manifesting the most symptoms on a particular day and enter it on the admitting sheet. For as long as all could remember, Jimmy Flynn had been attending the emergency department at regular intervals, with his major medical problems perhaps held in abeyance by the cheap red wine from a Kelowna hillside.

If there was one dark cloud on James Flynn's horizon, it came in the form of Miss Chapman, the head nurse at the emergency department. She had been in the department as long as anyone could remember, with crisp, starched uniform, nursing cap at the proper angle, and a Vancouver General Hospital nurse's pin dating back to the 1930s. If one would envision all of the characteristics of an old-time head nurse, they were personified in Miss Chapman's 5'8", full-bodied frame.

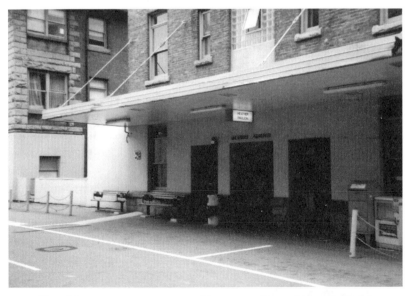

The old emergency entrance at Vancouver General Hospital holds indelible memories. James Flynn staggered regularly through these doors. Dr Stringer streaked naked from here one block to the doctor residence, the victim of an intern prank.

It was not that she was bad-tempered, mean-minded, harsh, or cranky, although at times she could be all of these; it was because she had in her mind the picture of an ideal emergency department which was clean, smelled of mayflowers, and was populated by properly uniformed, efficient nurses and interns who knew what they were doing. Patients in this ideal emergency ward were preferably clean, civil, sober, presenting only complaints that could be properly pigeonholed and dealt with.

James Flynn was the absolute contradiction to every aspect of this ideal condition. The very sight of James Flynn awakened every adverse trait in Miss Chapman's Presbyterian nature, and the expression of these would leave her feeling guilt for a week. Finally, for the peace of mind of the department and her own sanity, she decreed that James Flynn was not to be in the emergency department when she came on the scene in the morning.

When James shambled in or was carried in at 10:00 PM, the staff familiar with him would start an intravenous, give him some nourishment and vitamins, sober him up, and at 6:00 AM a breakfast, and he was sent out the door of the emergency department by 7:00 AM or at the very latest, 7:30.

Sometimes he would be linger as a new nurse failed to realize the importance of releasing him before eight o'clock, and Miss Chapman would come through the doors, sniff suspiciously, and cry out, "Is that disreputable James Flynn in my emergency again?"

James, who always had instincts of survival present, would leap from his stretcher, put on his battered felt hat, then take it off deferentially, and mutter, "A fine morning it is, Miss Chapman, and a good day to you. I think I'll be along at this time." All the while he would shuffle towards the exit door, pausing to gaze backwards at intervals and excuse himself.

Miss Chapman would stand up to her full height, point her finger at the rapidly disappearing form of James Flynn, and scream, "Don't you dare come to the Vancouver General Hospital again until you've had a wash and a shave and some new clothes, and don't you ever come back unless you're sober."

By this time, James had disappeared and was off into the morning weather to find something to lift his spirits, perhaps fitting him to be among the elect.

The elect, of course, as every Presbyterian knows, are those who have been pre-chosen by the Almighty to be delivered into heaven at the appointed time with no delays. Miss Chapman, I am sure, firmly believed that she was among the elect, and also equally firmly believed that James Flynn was not.

James Flynn, staunch "mick" that he was, probably had no idea what the elect were, and probably had no great desire to be numbered among them.

Time passed, and over the next two years of my term at the Vancouver General Hospital I was aware of the presence of James a number of times. As I ascended the training ladder, I visited the emergency department less frequently, but at these times my nostrils often picked up the sour, penetrating odour of a cross between sewer, cow barn, and winery, and hear the stertorous snorts and snores that could only belong to James Flynn. At these times I was conscious that the universe was evolving as it should, and the James Flynns of this life are part of the great scheme of things.

There were at that time two major hospitals in Vancouver who had very little in common, little communication between then, and certainly peculiar ideas of each other. These were Vancouver General and St. Paul's.

The Vancouver General Hospital thought of St. Paul's as being somewhat of a detached soup kitchen somewhere downtown and managed by pious nuns who sewed patches onto the breeches of the derelicts. Medical staff were thought to be elderly Irish physicians, practised in treating runny noses, foot rot, and hangovers.

St. Paul's Hospital regarded Vancouver General as a den of iniquity, with badly-trained nurses, probably wanton and of loose moral character — and who knew what went on in the after hours of that hospital? It was rumoured, they would claim, that the doctors mostly held qualifications from diploma mills down in Chicago and led a life of drink, gambling, and lecherous encounters with fast women.

Such were the prevailing attitudes of St. Paul's and Vancouver General Hospital. The fact that there could have been more communication was brought home to me a few years later when I met the head sister from the emergency department of St. Paul's Hospital. On an inspiration I asked her, "Would you know of a gentleman by the name of James Flynn in your emergency department?"

The head sister said, "James Flynn, why he hasn't missed our emergency department one week in the past ten years."

Still a bit suspicious, I continued, "Could this be the James Flynn that I might know? Did he have a little bit of an alcohol problem?"

"Alcohol problem," she commented, "I never saw him in my life that he wasn't drunk as a lord, and with that cheap booze, that Kelowna red, the whole hospital smelled."

I went on, "Would he be a little bit dirty, perhaps? Maybe he hadn't had a bath for a time?"

Replied the sister, "Dirty! He was worse than a pigpen in Derry. I don't think he had had a bath in forty years. He never shaved, he never washed, he never changed his clothes, and he smelled like the worst slop bucket in all of Ireland."

"Well, that is our James Flynn, you know," I said. "He was our patient, and he spent every third night in our emergency department for the last ten years."

"Your patient!" the sister exclaimed. "He was our patient. He spent every third night in our emergency department, and the next night he slept under the Granville Street Bridge — I always wondered where he spent that third night, and now I know."

I was struck with bemusement. It was then that I realized that the Granville Street Bridge was halfway between Vancouver General and St. Paul's. The traffic pattern was explained.

The sister continued, "Do you know what happened? Why, just last month we ran him out of our emergency department at half past seven just in time to miss the morning supervisor, and he went out

St. Pauls Emergency. James Flynn spent every third night here.

the door and collapsed right outside our emergency doors. We rushed out and put him on a stretcher, and he died right there, among all those who knew him and loved him. Like a saint, he died."

"Well," I said, "he was really our patient, and if he was getting the care that he should have over at St. Paul's, he would be with us still."

The sister answered, "*We* kept him alive all these years, and I am proud to say he died like a saint, and received last rites like a Christian gentleman, and even now the dear man is with his Lord, amen."

I said to myself, "Saints don't die like that in Vancouver General. As Chapman's elect, they are transported on a first class ticket directly into heaven." And then I thought, in heaven James Flynn wouldn't fit, and yet he wouldn't fit in hell either. He never hurt anyone but his own self. If he was among the elect, where would he go?

In James Flynn's heaven there would be two emergency departments joined by one bridge. He would be one night under the bridge, and the second and third in alternating emergency departments. Miss Chapman would make sure that he didn't overstay his time in either one.

CHAPTER 11

SHAUGHNESSY HOSPITAL, 1956

At the conclusion of my internship year at Vancouver General Hospital, I assessed my situation. My assets were one wife, one unborn child, one ancient Plymouth sedan, and a total accumulated debt of $300. Maybe I should have gone out in the real world and earned a proper living for my wife who had struggled through years of limited finances. My inclination, however, was to take further training, and to my surprise this was Marjorie's inclination also.

Marjorie's upbringing as a Salvation Army officer's kid was a definite asset here. She was not used to having money and had no particular ambitions to live in luxury. This was in contrast to the wives of other graduating doctors who wanted their husbands out building a lucrative medical practice and pursuing a more comfortable lifestyle.

I had a choice of continuing my training in surgery at Vancouver General Hospital or at Shaughnessy Hospital. To us it was vital to get the Shaughnessy post since it paid $25 a month more than did the one at Vancouver General Hospital. The difference between $175 a month and $150 a month was the difference between financial stability and financial disaster. We were determined not to borrow money from our parents, and if possible not from the bank either. Once we repaid the $300 owing to the scholarship fund at the University of Washington, we were out of debt. This may seem a minor point, but it meant an independence that many young doctors training now do not have.

In June we received notice that I had been accepted for the post of assistant surgical resident at Shaughnessy Hospital. With this news we moved into an ancient house on 21st Avenue close to Kingsway, a rather garishly painted structure belonging to a friendly, exuberant Italian named Lorenzo Spoletini. One of the terms of our lease was that he be allowed to continue pressing his grapes and making home-made wine in the back shed. This activity became very noticeable indeed two months later on warm evenings when fumes drifted through the neighbourhood, causing comments and complaints. However, with us a deal was a deal, and our landlord continued to make his wine, and we continued to fend off complaints from our neighbours.

The year at Shaughnessy was a pleasant one. There was a more relaxed atmosphere, the food was better, and there was a more philosophical approach taken to medicine. Perhaps this was because we were out of the strict academic atmosphere of the university, which had extended from my years in Seattle to the University of British Columbia role in the training program at Vancouver General.

Strictly speaking, Shaughnessy was a military hospital, complete with a Red Cross canteen. There were about 600 beds, some acute, some chronic care. I never begrudged the cost of this special facility. The veterans deserved every amenity for their sacrifice, which meant the sacrifice of potential for a successful civilian life. One old World War I veteran, Mr Bly, had held his ground when gas from a German attack rolled over his trench at the Somme. He gasped and choked every day of his life from those four hours spent representing his

Shaughnessy Hospital, 1st year surgical training 1956–1957.

country. People in Canada sacrificed, of course, but their payment was in work and money, and there is no comparison.

I had suffered little physical or emotional trauma in the war, but I understood these veterans and was at ease with them. I listened to their stories with awe and inwardly thanked God that I had been spared the horrors that many had experienced.

Attending medical staff were mostly specialists in their respective fields, often veterans of the Second World War. They were good teachers, and I profited greatly from listening to their wisdom.

One old-time orthopaedic surgeon I held in particular admiration. Hammy Boucher was big; a sports-minded man who had tramped through most of the rough country of British Columbia on camping expeditions, and who was very direct in attitude and speech. He worked hard and loathed people who were dishonest or malingerers.

Once in the out-patients department he examined a Korean war veteran, who came with a back complaint. Hammy decided that the man was faking and gave him a examination which was none too gentle, told him to get dressed, and sent him home with curt advice to get on with life, to get back to his job, and stop whining.

That night Hammy thought further on the man's complaints and at ten o'clock decided that he had been superficial and perfunctory in his assessment. He dressed, and in pouring rain, drove twenty-five miles from Vancouver to Richmond. There he knocked on the

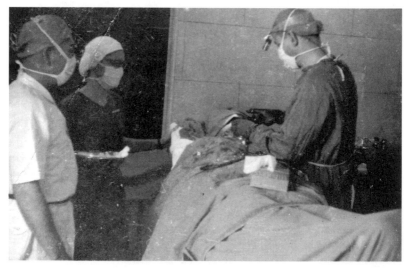

Novice surgeon Dr Lee's first tonsillectomy operation.

door and apologized to the dumbfounded patient. He asked the man to return the next day, and this time Hammy gave him the most thorough assessment possible. I am not sure what the outcome was, but certainly Hammy showed a humility which was much different from the gruff outward appearance that I had previously associated with him.

Hector Gillespie was another orthopaedic surgeon and team doctor for the Vancouver Lions football team. I found Hector to be a source of everyday common sense and he gave me many useful tips. He also bought me many bottles of Coca-Cola during our clinical times together.

Young people from the merchant marines often ended up at Shaughnessy Hospital. These were from foreign countries, and I well remember a young Dutch lad hospitalized after an accident on board his ship. He suffered a broken hip and had already been in Shaughnessy for three months when I saw him. Down the hall in another ward was a young woman who had incurred a broken leg while working on a Russian steamer. The two had often visited back and forth and in spite of the language barrier fell in love.

Alas, orthopaedic surgeons have a very low tolerance for in-hospital romances. When Dr Boucher found out about the blossoming relationship, he forbade all visiting between the two, and as quickly as possible had the young Dutch lad transferred to a different part of the hospital. I didn't agree with Hammy Boucher on all things and conspired with the nurses so that this separation was bridged. Who knows? Perhaps their recovery times were shortened by a little romance.

In Shaughnessy Hospital medical skill and knowledge was given a high priority, but personal integrity placed even higher. This was brought to my attention in rather stark terms. At 5:00 AM one November day I was called to emergency to examine an accident victim. The young man had an apparent fracture -dislocation of his ankle, and I recognized this as an emergency. After putting the ankle in a pillow cast I telephoned the chief resident doctor at his home. In spite of my anxiety, he ordered me to leave things be, and he would review it in the morning.

When Dr Boucher came around at 9:00 AM, and saw the nature of the injury, he was justly furious. He questioned his chief resident, demanding to know why this had not been attended to on admission to the hospital.

The resident doctor, perhaps first realizing the gravity of his error, claimed in defence that, "It was Lee's fault for not letting me know." I was shocked, but said nothing against the fabrication and took a proper dressing down from Hammy without replying.

Not much happened on the orthopaedic ward that Dr Boucher did not know, and he soon discovered the truth. From that time on he treated the offending resident like dirt, would not speak to him, and took from him all responsible work on the ward. The resident's career in orthopaedics was effectively dead; he would never get a recommendation, and no reputable hospital in Canada would accept him.

Dr Boucher made a great impression upon me. He was a hard man, but he was fair, and that is all I ask of anyone.

In the department of general surgery I was under the tutelage of Bill Sutherland, probably one of the finest surgeons in Canada. He was a surgeon of the old school, steady and competent under the most trying of circumstances. He showed an old-fashioned courtesy toward his colleagues and to his patients.

One day, one of Bill's colleagues came in critically stricken with a ruptured aneurysm of the aorta. It was Sutherland's awful responsibility to repair this, and through a long mid-line abdominal incision, in the face of massive hemorrhage, he put in stitch after stitch without the slightest change in his expression or tremor in his hands. It was through such example that we acquired the discipline to take our own place in horrifying times of crisis.

June of 1957 marked the finish of my ninth year since starting university. Gradually I was acquiring the skills and maturity to enter real world of medicine. In this world, one's responsibilities for the life and well-being of patients is not held lightly. Medicine is a strict task master and imposes a stern discipline on those who would be doctors.

For Marjorie and me and our young son Gerald it was a time for a respite from the academic arenas of medicine. This came about when I received an invitation to assist as locum tenens, or replacement doctor at Hazelton, BC, in a missionary hospital for the United Church. I was to receive $1000 a month plus housing, and this was a princely sum in those days. Marjorie and I looked at the offer of employment, hugged each other, and wrote back immediately with one question: When?

CHAPTER 12

HAZELTON DAZE

In July of 1957 I piloted my 1949 Plymouth over 700 miles of indifferent black top and gravel to the community of Hazelton, British Columbia. Hazelton is one of the more unique areas of BC, and in fact, while thought of as one city, is actually five communities all included in a three mile area.

The history of Hazelton goes back thousands of years. Prior to the arrival of the Caucasians, the natives gathered at Hazelton for commerce with the other tribes. The bountiful harvest of salmon from the Skeena River gave the local people a trade item that formed a stable supply for the surrounding tribes. In the 1860s there was an influx of whites. This was during the construction of the overland telegraph line from Washington State via Alaska and Siberia to Moscow. Unfortunately the project was discontinued when a telegraph line was laid across the Atlantic. Still, the wire extended as far as Hazelton, and indeed came to form the supporting structure of a Native-built bridge across the Bulkley River.

In the late 1800s paddle-wheel boats navigated the Skeena River from Prince Rupert to Hazelton, and these ships carried food supplies, mining equipment and passengers until the arrival of the railway in 1914.

Hazelton was also the site of several significant events in British Columbia's history. One of these was the thirteen-year pursuit of the fugitive Simon Gunanoot. Another was the famed New Hazelton bank robbery, one of the greatest shoot-outs in Canadian history. In this botched robbery attempt, four outlaws were killed, two others wounded, and a bank employee laid low. In 1995, Jessie Gould, hale and hearty at 87 years, described the event he saw and heard it at the time, through seven-year old eyes and ears. In this historical and interesting area I was introduced to the real-world practice of medicine.

The inhabitants of the Hazelton area were as interesting as its past history. There were eight Native villages in close proximity; two of these were Carrier or Athabascan speaking and six Tsimshian. The latter were centred at Hazelton and stretch from Kispiox to the coast. An interesting relic from the past were small grave houses in the cemetery overlooking Old Hazelton. Some of these were quite elaborate and, at one time, included food and clothing for the journey to the afterworld. This burial custom was abandoned years prior to my arrival, but a number of the structures still stand, most in disrepair.

The language of the Tsimshian was totally incomprehensible to the Carriers, and vice versa. The usual language of communication between villages and tribes was Chinook, the lingua franca extending from Oregon to Alaska, and into Alberta.

Other inhabitants were a mixture, some Asians from the mining days, some pioneer families from the 1800s, still engaged in farming, logging, or commerce, and a number of people who could only be described as individuals who did not fit in more settled areas of the province. These were often elderly, reclusive types, who lived in their small holdings and log cabins, year in and year out, with minimal outside socializing.

The five distinctive communities composing Hazelton nestled under the shadow of the 7000-foot Rocher de Boule mountain peak immediately to the south. South Hazelton was the most northerly, New Hazelton, a mile south, was the railway centre, and across the Bulkley River Old Hazelton lay enclosed by the junction of the Skeena and Bulkley Rivers. There was another community called Two Mile, halfway between the towns of New Hazelton and Old Hazelton. The fifth community, Wrinch Memorial, or Hazelton Memorial Hospital seemed to have an identity of its own. The personnel settled about the hospital, and for the most part had immigrated from some other place. Many of the nurses were from eastern Canada, often from the Maritimes.

The head nurse was an unflappable and capable nurse, originally from England. There were also a number of practical nurses who had not gone through nursing school, but had a year's formal training in large hospitals. Most of these were from western Canada.

Besides me, there were two other doctors, Dr Whiting, a graduate of the University of Toronto, and Dr Palmer from the University of Western Ontario in London. The oldest, Dr Whiting, was cheerful and seemed to know a good deal about the background of the Natives. His rolling gait made him a natural woodsman and he delighted in spending time camping or undertaking an expedition into the wild with a party of the more adventuresome nurses. Dr Palmer had some military experience but, while competent in medicine, was obviously tuned to urban life more than rural. I fitted in reasonably well, since I had been raised in central British Columbia, knew the Chinook language from my Cariboo upbringing, and felt at home in smaller cities.

The hospital had three floors, the top being allotted to maternity and children, the next was the medical and surgical floor, and the main floor was the laboratory, dining room, and administration. Doctor's offices were also on the main floor. The fifty-bed hospital was filled in wintery, blustery times, but in good summer weather was often half empty.

The doctors resided on the hospital grounds. Marjorie and I had a commodious apartment, while Dr Whiting and Dr Palmer had houses nearby. In a field adjacent to the hospital was a nine-hole golf course. This proved to be a happy location, since on-duty nurses

Opposite: Native graves, Hazelton, BC.

could dash to the second floor and wave a white sheet to summon doctors who might be golfing.

Most of the medical work was accomplished in the hospital, but once or twice a week, and this was a carry-over from times of limited transportation, afternoon clinics were manned in the outlying Native villages.

I was used to the furious activity of big city hospitals, and was surprised at the relaxed pace in Hazelton. Rarely did we have serious emergencies, which was fortunate, because it was very difficult for us to transport patients with complicated problems. The nearest airport was 40 miles away, and the nearest advanced-treatment hospital was 500 miles away by air. The CN railway ran east and west, and it was only possible to send patients to Edmonton by rail, a journey of a day and a half.

I had a year of post-graduate surgical training, and ordinary procedures such as appendectomies, tonsillectomies, and the treatment of fractures, and other trauma were within my capabilities. During my two years at Hazelton, two women out of a hundred required a Caesarean section, one of which I did. The other woman, our matron, was referred to Vancouver.

Life on the hospital grounds proceeded at an even, relaxed pace. The doctors had lunch at home each day, office hours were in the after-noon, and once a week a chapel service was held at the small church on the hospital grounds. Usually one of the other doctors led this service.

An easy relationship developed between the doctors, particularly between Dr Whiting and me, since we shared a classical education in Latin. Nurses were our sisters in medicine, but a traditional formal relationship existed between the doctors and nurses. When a doctor arrived on the ward, the nurses stood at attention, and a nurse always accompanied the doctor on the rounds to see the patients. I think this relation-ship made for both better doctors and nurses than a less formal relationship does. It did not mean that the nurses were inferior to doctors. A mutual respect developed between the two, which was reinforced by this old-fashioned discipline.

The patients regarded the medical practitioners with respect. This confidence had a decided therapeutical benefit. Indeed, in the days before the era of modern medicines, therapy was largely accomplished by the personality of the doctor and the confidence and respect in which he was held by patients. There were very few effective medicines before 1940.

Overall, Hazelton welcomed Marjorie and me and we felt at home and part of the community of all five small towns and eight Native villages. Indeed I soon knew almost every man, woman, and child by name, and also the dogs, cats, horses, and cows. I also made it a point to become acquainted with the reclusive men and women in their isolated cabins. In Hazelton, I found the work for which I had trained for nine years, and I felt happy and contented at last.

Wrinch Memorial Hospital, Hazelton. (Courtesy Jessie Gould).

CHAPTER 13

MEDICAL SERVICES AT WRINCH MEMORIAL HOSPITAL

I was initiated to the practice of medicine in Wrinch Memorial Hospital in Hazelton. This was a happy coincidence, since I always had a sensitivity for history. Indeed, the history of this establishment went back to 1900, and was closely entwined with the local establishment of the church and the development of ties between the eight adjacent Native tribes and the white settlers. Central to the development of the hospital was transportation, first by steamship from Prince Rupert 180 miles to the west and following that, the construction of the Grand Trunk Pacific Railway. The hospital assumed a disproportionate role in north-central British Columbia, and became a second Mayo Clinic, even founding its own school of nursing.

Dr Wrinch, a Methodist missionary doctor, had arrived in the Hazelton area in 1898 with his new bride, a nurse/deaconess. Apparently it took them six weeks to make the journey from the Coast to cover 200 miles of the Skeena River by canoe. The discrepancy between the time and length of this journey might be ascribed to the distractions a young, honeymooning couple may have experienced in such breath-taking scenery, or to the difficulties of transportation. While swarms of biting flies, mosquitoes, and "no-see-ums" usually hastened travellers on their way, an idyllic journey of two people in love may have created a bond which defied the hardships of travel and the annoyances of the insect world.

Following the establishment of a clinic at Kispiox ten miles north of Hazelton, Dr Wrinch found that this location was not central enough to best serve the needs of the communities, and moved his headquarters to an escarpment on the wedge of land between the junction of the Bulkley and Skeena Rivers. This was about a half mile from the banks of the Skeena and the centre of Old Hazelton. In 1902 the first hospital was built using Dr Wrinch's architectural skills. Nearby gardens and provisions for animal husbandry were established to supply the needs of the hospital.

Under the slogan, "Every young lady a nurse," he established the school of nursing in 1904. By "every young lady a nurse" he did not mean every young female in the community. The actual requirements applied to a small portion of local young women, that is, those who had some education, were white, and from a good family. Each September from 1904 till 1932, a nursing class entered Hazelton's hospital and three years later graduated as fully qualified nurses with distinctive pin, nurse's cap, and cloak. I was gratified to find that the last six classes took a final year at the Vancouver General School of Nursing. Indeed, the head nurse of the orthopaedic ward of Shaughnessy Hospital was a graduate of the Hazelton Nursing School.

With construction of the railway in 1914, Hazelton Hospital became a well-stocked medical centre complete with one of the first x-ray machines installed in a northern BC hospital. And over four decades later I was pleased to find a store of instruments far beyond the usual allotment to a primary care hospital.

Surgical instruments were in keeping with the big-city hospital, and retractors, forceps, and needle drivers were in plentiful supply and of a variety rarely found in a small hospital.

In the maternity ward I found a variety of obstetrical forceps equal to the inventory at Vancouver General Hospital. Even complicated deliveries were handled in Hazelton rather than being shipped to Edmonton or Vancouver. The orthopaedic instruments

The founder of modern medicine in Hazelton, Dr Horace Wrinch. His example influenced my career. Painting presented to hospital by his three sisters.

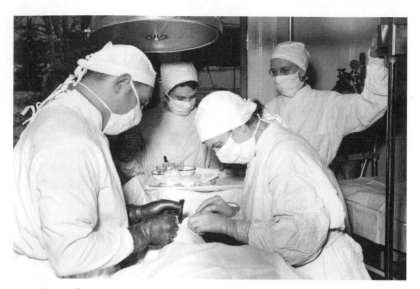

Surgical team at work, Wrinch Memorial Hospital. Dr Violet Markin Surgeon, Dr Raynhem assisting, nurse Jones giving the patient open drop ether as an anesthetic, and nurse MacLeod (Courtesy C.L. Botham)

were in good supply with hammers, drills, different types of fixation equipment, and the latest in pins. From these instruments I gathered that the orthopaedic practice was sophisticated, likely due to the rough and ready activities of the men pushing railways and highways through difficult, mountainous country.

When I looked into the pharmacy, a large room on the first floor of the hospital, I could not help but gasp in amazement. Shelf after shelf held gallon jugs containing elixirs, medications, herbal remedies, and almost anything one could imagine as a medication or mixture from a pre-modern, pharmaceutical age.

I delighted in mixing up preparations of basic herbal medications, to combine their different physiological properties. The active medicine was mated with syrup of cherry or syrup of strawberry, or something else. Most medicines are formed on an alkaloid base which has a very bitter taste.

One formulation for asthma and colds was so effective that a grateful patient came back and asked me to mix up two or three more bottles for him. Unfortunately no two of my mixtures were the same, and I could only approximate his first prescription.

In surveying the equipment and pharmacy of the Hazelton Memorial Hospital, I could not help but admire the skill and knowledge demonstrated in medical practice on the frontier. In some ways they were ahead of their time.

One of the graduates of the nursing school in the early twenties came back twenty years later and recounted the story of how Dr Wrinch had received word of a seriously ill, young woman in the village of Kitwanga 30 miles to the west. In deep winter, he had harnessed up a dog team, made the journey to Kitwanga on the frozen river, packed the stricken young woman on his sleigh, and brought her back to the hospital.

She likely had an internal hemorrhage from a ruptured pregnancy. On returning to the hospital Dr Wrinch had tea, then, with the matron giving an anaesthetic, opened his patient's abdomen, removed the offending tubal pregnancy, poured in three litres of sterile salt solution, and closed up the abdomen again. This apparently was all in a day's work. Frequently he went miles by dog team or sleigh, sometimes sleeping in the sleigh while an assistant drove through the night hours.

I resolved to show as much fortitude and skill as possible and to follow in the footsteps of this giant of a man who had preceded me in Hazelton.

Dr Wrinch utilized a dog team like this for house calls. (Courtesy Jessie Gould)

CHAPTER 14

NATIVE MEDICINE
AND HOME REMEDIES

There were 3500 Native people grouped around Hazelton when I arrived and I had some opportunity to learn of the Native medical treatments and medicines. The art of medicine was not highly developed in British Columbia, perhaps due to the smaller tribes and also to the dispersal of people into small groups common in a hunting and fishing society. Agriculture and animal husbandry were never a factor among the western tribes.

Some herbal medicines were applied and there is indication that willow bark, which contains salicylates, the basic component of aspirin, was used. Aside from this there was probably no effective medicine known to them. Spruce pitch or gum was mixed with lard and applied to sores. Burn holes were used to treat rheumatoid arthritis, and steam huts addressed respiratory conditions. Oolichan grease was the panacea for the tribes along the coast and a medication the interior tribes acquired through barter. In former times, the native people depended on the shamans who relied mainly on rituals and hypnotism for their treatment.

By in large, medical treatments were ineffective by western medical standards, and by the time I arrived in Hazelton, the aboriginal medicinal treatments had largely been discarded.

This abandonment was perhaps premature, as salicylates have proven to be a very effective drug for pain, fevers, and as a protection against heart attacks and strokes. Salicylates are extracted quite readily from willow bark, and indeed, their position in herbal medicine goes back to Hippocrates' time, over 2300 years ago. Acetaminophen and codeine superseded willow bark, perhaps to the detriment of the natives' health.

Pitch gum ointment was of some use, and I remember Dr Whiting climbing up a spruce tree to get spruce gum for an old native who placed great faith in this treatment.

The burn holes used for arthritis were affected in the following manner. Dry willow sticks were burned, and when the ends were glowing, the ember was applied to the arthritic joint. This resulted in a third degree burn one centimetre in diameter, which invariably became infected. It may be that the increased heat and blood flow caused by this burn improved the arthritis, but the overall result was an infected burn which, in my experience, was detrimental. I have seen as many as four burn holes on the knee, and all were infected. We dealt with the residue of this treatment with antibiotic ointment and penicillin.

The panacea for all the natives in the Hazelton area was oolichan grease. This had some pharmacological basis for effectiveness, as it contained a large amount of vitamin A and D. Its preparation was of interest. From the masses of oolichan, also called candlefish that ran up the Nass river, tons were taken and piled on a concave rock face and left in the sunshine. With the heat and putrefaction, the oil settled out and was collected in handmade square cedar boxes containing about fifty pounds. These boxes were carried inland over what became known as the Grease Trail as a trade item.

Oolichan grease was used for a variety of conditions, and in my time was still freely used for things such as croup or coughs. It was also recommended for rheumatism, arthritis, kidney infections, liver upset, indigestion, constipation, infertility, frigidity, nymphomania, impotence, and general infirmities of the aged.

Shamans were no longer commonly used, but, they still had a role in treating the ill. I had the opportunity to witness this on one occasion. Early in my stay at Hazelton, a young woman presented herself. She was agitated, withdrawn, depressed, and babbling out a story of an owl sitting on her window the previous night. Dr Whiting informed me that this was the result of a shaman casting a spell on her. He recommended that she be treated by a good shaman, and indeed, this eventually was necessary, since modern medicines did not seem to affect any improvement.

The shaman, dressed in feathers and robes, circled around the withdrawn and incoherent patient, rubbing a feather-plumed staff across her body, then shaking it outside the open window. The young

Houston Tommy in ritual attire was known as a good shaman.

woman recovered soon after this.

The owl seemed to have a place in the native beliefs and was reckoned to be a messenger of bad news. I knew from my youth that Natives in the Williams Lake area often kept their camp fires going all night, and their lights on as long as possible, to ward off the evil spirits speaking through the owl.

It may well be that there is a gap in western medicine that the shaman might fill. I have noted that modern, scientific, medicine deals very effectively with such things as pneumonia, tonsillitis, appendicitis, fractures, skin eruptions, and other conditions where medical or surgical treatments are the primary therapeutic method.

Western medicine deals rather poorly with a number of conditions which can only be described as the wounds and maladies of the stresses of our daily living. Certainly, doctors' offices are crowded with people who are treated with psychoactive or sedating medications over and over, without much benefit. In fact, if this group were separated from an average medical practitioner's clientele, fewer doctors would be required in our society.

The native peoples across North America may have acted hastily in relinquishing their traditional medical practices. White doctors rarely prescribe effective replacements. Neither the aboriginal peoples, nor the government purses, are helped by excessive use of sedatives, tranquilizers, analgesics and mood-altering substances.

Opposite: The owl often figured in Native superstitions and was thought by natives to bear bad tidings.

CHAPTER 15

MEDICAL POTPOURRI

Albert Einstein is quoted as saying that when the answer to an unsolvable problem comes intuitively, then one is in the presence of God. I have often stood in awe of the complexities of the human make-up, and the difficulty in finding the elusive factors that mesh the workings of personality, genetics, the disease process and environment.

Often answers come intuitively rather than through cold, scientific reasoning, perhaps because of many past experiences. The impact of experiences are mediated through one's own life, clinical training, special aptitudes, and skills.

In medical school and hospital training positions, the young doctor has a good deal of work and some responsibility, but this responsibility is limited. The ultimate responsibility lies always with someone higher up the chain. In medical practice, the awful weight of responsibility falls on the practitioner's shoulders. A wise doctor, nearing the end of his practice, observed: "Two people can always carry a coffin better than one," meaning that if one was caring for a seriously ill patient, a second opinion was always wise. Looking back over my introduction to private, general practice, I sometimes elicited a second opinion unnecessarily, but more often I was both strengthened and heartened by the advice of a more mature colleague.

Ruby was a young woman with a baffling illness. She was, as many young women seemed to be in the Tsimshian tribes, a princess. She had been working in the fish industry in Prince Rupert and returned to Hazelton on her way to the native village of Kispiox. She complained of a temperature, a sore throat, and a general feeling of unwellness. Examination showed an ill young woman with reddened throat. Because her temperature was 101° F, I admitted her to hospital and gave her penicillin. This treatment would correct the problem in over ninety-nine percent of the cases, but the next day Ruby had not improved; in fact she was worse, her temperature was 102° F, her neck was stiff and sore, and she had generalized aching of muscles. The treatment seemed to be the correct one, but the following day her temperature was 103° F, and her condition more serious. I tried to find out her past medical history, and there was some evidence from relatives that she had been admitted to Miller Bay Hospital, a tuberculosis hospital at Prince Rupert. This admission could not be immediately confirmed, and indeed there were no signs she had ever had tuberculosis.

I reassured the family that she should improve shortly, but this did not happen and I myself was startled one day to find a bright new casket pushed into one corner of her room. My optimism faded, and I spoke to Dr Whiting about the situation.

His advice, after examining her, was to go after the Miller Bay people for an in-depth report of her past treatment. Sure enough, this revealed a confirmed history of tuberculosis. My uncertainty was cleared completely when an examination of spinal fluid showed gross pus. Ruby had tuberculous meningitis, which proved to be fatal.

Not all cases of tuberculosis ended so tragically. Peter was a case in point. One day I met this cheerful, slim native man, about fifty years of age. He was walking down the streets of Hazelton, but awkwardly. I inquired why he was limping, and he replied that he had had a sore foot for the previous two months. I told Peter to come up to the hospital, where an x-ray revealed a punched out lesion of the bone in his heel. Further tests showed that it was a tuberculous infection.

I referred him to the tuberculosis hospital at Miller Bay for treatment and a couple of years later, while walking the streets of Hazelton, bumped into the same cheerful individual. "Peter," I said, "how are you?"

"Oh, very well, Doctor," he replied. "You fixed me up — hardly took any time."

Remembering the slow resolution of tuberculous bone lesions I said, "Oh, how long did it take, Peter?"

He replied, "Oh, hardly any time, Doctor, only seventeen months."

Big Tommy Michelle belongs in the annals of medicine. Prior to my arrival at Hazelton, Big Tommy developed cancer of the stomach. He was sent to Vancouver where surgery confirmed the diagnosis, and he was sent home to die. But Big Tommy did not die. To every one's amazement, he recuperated and went through the years without any trace of his illness.

I examined him for something trivial, and happened to glance through his past medical records, and sure enough, there were operating reports and biopsy reports confirming his cancer of the stomach. I examined him from head to toe, and not a single trace of cancer remained. I followed his status for the two years I was in Hazelton and then, kept in touch by correspondence following my departure. Big Tommy did not develop any reoccurrence of his cancer and went on to die several years later of natural causes. There is no medical explanation for this. The diagnosis was confirmed by biopsy. He should have died, but he did not.

During my second winter at Hazelton there was an epidemic of whooping cough. This struck Prince Rupert earlier, then travelled up the Skeena River, arriving at Hazelton in February. An epidemic should have been avoided with immunization shots, but many people, including babies, failed to get immunized, and a number who had received shots got the whooping cough anyway. The time-honoured method of treatment among the Natives was the use of oolichan grease, but this plainly did not work, and in a number of the

two-and-under infants died in the Prince Rupert area. At Hazelton we developed a method of treatment with early hospitalization, intravenous fluids, antibiotics, and vitamins. We did not lose a single baby during the whooping cough epidemic, but all of them whooped until spring.

Weddings are usually a source of excitement and happiness, particularly to the young bride. Thus it was that the wedding day of Marianne was eagerly awaited. On the slated Saturday morning, I received an agitated call from the bride-to-be. She had awakened in the morning with a wry neck and head tilted awkwardly to the side. This gave her a good deal of discomfort and difficulty in speaking. Could I do anything about this in the four hours remaining before the wedding?

I brought her into the clinic, had her lie on a flat table, and, with my nurse holding her feet, firmly seized her chin and the back of her head. With gradually increasing traction the head was rotated from side to side. There was a snap, and lo and behold, the neck and head were aligned once more.

She walked down the aisle on the arm of her father, radiant as a bride should be, gave her wedding vows clearly, and returned down the aisle with her new husband in a shower of rice and good wishes. I thought that I presented an unlikely figure for a Cupid, but there it was. I haven't bad-mouthed a chiropractor since.

Opposite: The Village of Hazelton, Skeena River. (Jesse Gould)

CHAPTER 16

AN OLD WEST DISASTER

In medical life, moments of tension arise from seemingly placid and innocuous beginnings. Thus it was at Wrinch Memorial Hospital in Hazelton, one Wednesday morning in September, 1958.

Medical rounds were over, the usual runny ears of young children viewed with frustration, the arthritic conditions attended to, the coughs, the sneezes, the rashes, the cases of indigestion dealt with, and finally the awaited morning coffee time arrived.

At Wrinch Memorial the three doctors, together with the head nurse and whatever other nurses were free, met in the kitchen where coffee was served along with fresh pastry. This ritual was about to be observed in time-honoured fashion when the telephone in the nearby doctor's office rang insistently.

The succinct message shocked us. A native family some twenty miles down the Skeena River toward Kitwanga was travelling to a blueberry patch by team and wagon. The team, thought to be gentle and well-trained, were startled by a grouse on the side of the narrow road and bolted. Sitting on the front seat were a father, mother, and a two-year old child. A seven-year old child in the back of the wagon was immediately thrown.

The tongue of the wagon, dividing the horses and attached in a ring from the neck yoke, dropped, and the horses in their mad flight caught the tongue against a tree. This flipped the wagon end over end, to come crashing down on the rough sun-baked ground.

When alarmed friends arrived soon after, the extent of the tragedy was apparent at once. The mother was dead, as was the seven-year old child. The two-year old was missing, and the father lay beside the wagon, completely paralyzed from the shoulders down. He could only move his thumb and first finger on either hand, and he breathed, weakly.

We heard this burdensome news in the telephone call from the small Native village of Kitwanga and instructed the caller to bring the father to the hospital, taking all precautions to protect his neck. Also he was to inform the Mounted Police to start a search for the two-year old child. At the hospital, we assembled a stretcher, intravenous lines, and Mastoid tongs with head weights to deal with the suspected fractured neck and paralysis.

In approximately an hour's time, a van drove up to the emergency entrance. In the back of the van was a heavy-set native man who we knew well. It was obvious that he had almost complete paralysis from the neck down. About the same time the two-year old daughter arrived. She had been found wandering in the woods about a quarter mile from the wreckage of the wagon. She was stunned and traumatized, but apparently not seriously injured.

With severe neck injuries, shock is often present, and Thomas had not escaped this complication. Intravenous drips were started, and tongs much like ice tongs were placed against the mastoid bone of the skull immediately back of each ear, and sixteen pounds of weight applied to extend the neck as much as possible. This traction was counter-balanced with weights extending through pulleys back over the foot of the bed.

A disaster of this magnitude is beyond feeling. What must be done, however, should be done, and as efficiently as possible. Contact was made with a neurosurgeon in Vancouver, some 700 miles away, with plans made for transporting Thomas some 40 miles to the nearest airport and then evacuating him to Vancouver. Because Thomas was in shock, this trip was to be delayed for twenty-four hours.

During this time, Thomas's condition deteriorated. He was a heavy man, and his chest soon showed evidence of early pneumonia, his abdomen bloated, a result of the trauma and shock.

By the next morning, word had travelled through the entire community and native village. His departure for Vancouver approached, and the ambulance arrived at the door of the hospital. By that time there were thirty to forty native people, from the elders to young folk, gathered around the ambulance. Thomas was brought through the front door of the hospital, and friends carried the stretcher to the ambulance.

The crowd was tearful on seeing one of their own going far away from his home and family. About the only movement Thomas could make was to raise and lower his eyelids, and as he did so, tears coursed freely down his cheeks.

We all felt that it was near the end for Thomas, but his best chance, though slim, was to be transferred to a neuro-surgical unit. Although we expressed optimism that he would return, the native people were not misguided and their eyes held little hope. Suddenly from the eldest came a wailing sound, a haunting lament which was picked up by all assembled. Amid the wails and grief, Thomas was lifted into the ambulance, and the slow journey began along the main highway to the airport. As long as the ambulance was in sight, the wails continued, starting at one spot and rising to its highest pitch, then fading off to a thin keening that harkened to all the sorrow felt by each individual.

The medical people knew chances were slim but hoped for that small possibility of success. The native people had no hope for Thomas. When a man ends up dead from the shoulders down from an incident on an innocent berry-picking expedition, that man's day has come. When a husband sits by his wife and children in a wagon, the neck yoke falls, the team runs away, and the family is destroyed, that is the sign that his day has come. So it was with Thomas. Two days later he joined his wife and child and was buried at Kitwanga.

Sorrow and wailing are fitting; no outside medical help will change the event. The great spirit has spoken.

CHAPTER 17

LITTLE LOST HIPPIE BOY

If Little Joe Peters had been born a few years later, he would have been a flower child or a hippie.

Home was basic, a rural log cabin without running water or electricity. An outhouse sat near the edge of a small clearing.

Little Joe's mother fit the picture of a flower child, complete with granny glasses and a long, flowered skirt that had rarely seen a washtub and never an iron. She had the proper credentials; a master's degree from San Francisco State in California. Joe's father was tall, slim, wore a checkered shirt open at the neck, and had blond hair done up in a queue. He was a poet. The tax-payers of Canada had a healthy stake in the Peters family; they were supported by welfare.

Parenting was apparently not one of their strengths. Little Joe, at age eight, was skinny, his long, blonde hair unkempt and tangled. He showed no evidence of having been washed on a regular basis.

He first appeared in my office at The Wrinch Memorial Hospital after a social worker visited his home. Little Joe had survived his eight years without benefit of immunizations, vaccinations, or any sort of medical care.

He did not come our way due to any serious disease, but because of his teeth. When he reluctantly opened his mouth, we saw that he had not known dental care during his lifetime. His gums had receded to the roots of his teeth, and these roots were easily seen. This was no doubt a result of neglect and perhaps lack of vitamins and a proper diet. His teeth required extraction, and he was admitted to hospital with the plan that necessary dental work would be done under anaesthetic.

Opposite: Last farewell for Thomas.

Little Joe looked sad and lost as his mother steered up to the children's ward, and when she left that chilly November evening, he looked after her, a haunting, forlorn expression on his thin face. He was not used to an easy life, but the isolated cabin was the only home he knew, and provided key commodities: security and family.

Like many children who have had a hard existence, he did not cry for his mother. At supper time he ate everything placed before him and at eight o'clock, Katie Friesen, the night nurse, tucked him into bed. He seemed to settle down as the unfamiliar electric lights were turned off.

Up to this point Little Joe was much like many other children under similar circumstances; this was to change. At nine o'clock Nurse Friesen called my home, and in an alarmed voice, said that Little Joe was missing. She had searched the ward and other nurses had scoured the entire hospital. He had disappeared, and the only conclusion was that he had left the hospital, clad only in his pajamas.

This was particularly worrisome, since the November night was cold, and a skiff of snow lay on the frozen ground. A half moon rose low in the sky, shedding a feeble light over the leafless trees. The hospital was set out on a semi-wooded slope, half a mile from the village of Hazelton, and three miles from a second community. There was only a scattering of homesteads carved out of the wooded area around us.

Everyone nearby was alerted, the police notified, and dozens of people hunted the woods and the road leading to the boy's home, fifteen miles up the Kispiox Valley.

With luck, a single barefoot print was found in the snow between the hospital and the main road and concluded Little Joe was heading home. Every minute counted, but 10:30 and 11:00 PM came, and still no evidence of the lost stray. The searchers grew more frantic.

A half mile from the hospital, a narrow side road wound through a small grouping of houses back into the mountains. On this road lived a reclusive old bachelor in a small cabin. Mr McDames' closest friend was his mongrel dog. That night, this dog became a hero. Soon after he was let out the cabin door for his late night "piddle," he began to bark insistently. His master opened the door, walked out a few paces, and in the light of the waning moon saw a small, bent-over form shuffling up the trail.

Opposite: Kispiox Valley log cabin. Little Joe was raised here.

Mr McDames hurried as fast as he could, and was able to get nearer the small hiker, who did not stop, but continued to plod along his path toward the darkened woods. McDames caught the boy in mid-stride, picked him up and held him close. The shivering waif did not struggle, nor did he cry or speak, but after a few seconds threw his arms around the bony chest of the elderly man and clung tightly.

It was our little Joe Peters. From his frosty pajamas it was clear to us that he had made his way from the hospital to the darkened path where by chance he was found. Mr McDames wrapped the boy in a coat, held him close and walked to the main road where searchers greated the elderly recluse. In this cluster of adults, for the first time our little fugitive whimpered and then broke into muffled sobs.

The joy and relief felt by everyone could not be described. Little Joe was warmed, he was hugged, he was petted. For the first time in his life he was fussed over. He could have been lost and frozen to death, but now he was found and safe.

His frostbitten feet were red and swollen for a few days, but healed surprisingly quickly. Next, his teeth were treated, but best of all, the community rallied around this unlikely family. Time proved that the support and caring made a difference in their lives.

A month later, sturdier and less wary, Little Joe, clad in warm clothing, attended school for the first time. In spite of his shyness, he seemed to appreciate being a local hero.

Opposite: Little Joe left through this door of the hospital and made his way up the frozen road above.

CHAPTER 18

THE DISTEMPER OF THE SALVATION ARMY LIEUTENANT

Traditionally, the churches around Hazelton enjoyed a pre-eminence in their locale. The Salvation Army attended to the spiritual needs of most inhabitants of Kitseguecla twenty miles west of Hazelton and the Natives of Glen Vowell six miles east of Hazelton. The village of Hazelton was served by both the Salvation Army and by the Anglican Church.

The village of Hazelton was manned, or should I say "womanned", by two young Salvation Army Lieutenants, both officers with their first charge. One was cheerful, chubby, competent, and fun to be with, while the other was more reserved, but dedicated to the Lord's work. Both were held in affection by their group of stalwart members and adherents in the village. My wife Marjorie, brought up in the Salvation Army, formed a warm relationship with the two officers, and they invited us to tea on several occasions.

On one of these visits we met their huge tan dog who had an uncertain pedigree but an amiable disposition. Since I am a dog lover, the two of us formed a friendly relationship, and whenever I passed by the Salvation Army headquarters this massive mutt would come out, greet me warmly, and wait to be petted.

This mundane bit of history became the backdrop for a catastrophic series of events. At that time there was no veterinarian in the Hazelton area, and most of the dogs were not vaccinated against distemper. The situation soon changed, however, as distemper swept through the district, and almost every dog became a victim. I was pressed into service giving penicillin, which seemed to pull a number of the mutts and mongrels through, but almost every unvaccinated pure-blood dog in the district died.

One night I received a concerned call from the Army lieutenant that their dog had gone mad, and could I please come immediately. In the meantime they would take precautions and keep a safe distance from the animal.

I seized my medical bag, started the car, and made my way from the hospital grounds the mile into Hazelton. The lights were on in the Salvation Army quarters, and anxious faces appeared at the window.

The lieutenants opened the door, bustled me in, and pointed up the stairs to the second floor. "He's there; he's gone mad. He probably has hydrophobia. Be careful, whatever you do." At that time "hydrophobia" was a common term for rabies.

I reassured the young lieutenants, seized my bag, and went up the stairs to visit my old canine friend, who was now a canine patient. There he stood at the top of the stairs, rigid, stiff, every hair on his dun coat bristling on end. Between slobbers he uttered quavering, mournful howls.

The situation required drastic steps. I suspected that this was actually distemper rather than hydrophobia, and the lieutenants came up the stairs, stood on either side of their pet, while I gave a hefty intra-muscular injection of a sedative. After five minutes the dog relaxed and fell over into a deep sleep. Penicillin was soon injected and on this note the lieutenants made tea. A further check on their pet revealed a sleeping animal with stable breathing and heartbeat.

Salvation army Lieutenant and flock.

Next day the Army informed me that the patient had slightly improved. I made another house call, gave another shot of penicillin, and the canine recovered completely within a week.

So far the story is heart-warming, but the next chapter was anything but. About six weeks later one of the officers consulted me for treatment of a puzzling illness. Sharp pains in her lower limbs, involving feet and ankles, had persisted for several days and she noted some weakness in her foot movements. Conditions such as multiple sclerosis, spinal tumours, and lower peripheral neuritis were possibilities. Because of the severe pain she was admitted to hospital and given pain relievers, but within a day required morphine. Each day the level of paralysis advanced centrally and the pains remained constant and severe. Assessment of spinal fluid showed marked increase in the level of protein, and after some further thought and examination it seemed that the young woman had Guillain-Barré syndrome, a form of neuritis. The pains were up to the thigh by this time, and each day there was a corresponding advancement of the paralysis.

In alarm I called a neurologist in Vancouver and discussed the case at some length. He assured me that the progression usually stopped, and reversal of the disease process occurred. I was not entirely comforted, and asked if this condition ever resulted in paralysis of respirations. He replied matter-of-factly, "Oh yes, occasionally we see this."

Thinking of our position 500 air miles away from an efficient respirator, I said, "What, you mean that she can stop breathing?"

"Oh yes," he replied in the same tone.

"She'll be on her way down as soon as we can get her there." I said.

This would not be easy since we were 150 miles away from Prince Rupert and an air ambulance. The closest airport, at Smithers, was not operating.

Our local ambulance and the young lieutenant set out for Prince Rupert but the roads were snowed in at Terrace, and an overnight stay was necessary there. The next day, with the roads cleared, she was taken to Prince Rupert, where an ancient Catalina flying boat evacuated her to the Queen Charlotte Island airport of Sandspit. From there she was transported to Vancouver General Hospital.

At this point her luck changed; she began to recover, and was sent back to Hazelton after three weeks. No sooner had she arrived, than process repeated itself, and she began to experience peripheral pain and paralysis again. However, this time we toughed it out in Hazelton, and she went on to make a full recovery.

Did the mad dog of the Salvation Army lassies cause the lieutenant's problems? Likely so. Guillain-Barré syndrome often follows a viral illness. I only know that the lieutenant and her doctor should gain an extra star when they reach the promised land. Perhaps there will even be a star left over for a tan-coated mutt who likely started the whole adventure with his canine distemper.

CHAPTER 19

RESURRECTION AT KITWANGA FLATS

"**D**oc, how would you like to go on a little trip? Get your bag, and we'll be around in twenty minutes." This came from Corporal Dodds of the Royal Canadian Mounted Police (RCMP) on a chilly night in February. I was in the midst of my evening cocoa, my one-year old youngster fast asleep, and a loving young wife cuddled next to me on the sofa preparing for bedtime and sweet dreams.

The obvious answer was, "No, not on your life! Get lost! I don't do house calls in isolated villages thirty miles away." I internalized this response, and replied that I would be ready.

Sure enough, in twenty minutes the RCMP van with Corporal Dodds and a constable drew up beside our residence door on the hospital grounds, and I picked up my bag and climbed into the back seat. As we started out, I learned the details of this strange request. A young native by the name of Oscar, whom I knew vaguely from several previous visits, had shot himself. I was not surprised since Oscar had indicated that he might be a menace to himself or others in the community. In fact, he had been picked up for threatening others at a local dance some time before.

As it was winter and late at night, there was no chance of taking the main highway west and crossing by ferry to the Kitwanga village, and so we were forced to take the back road down the north side of the Skeena River. This gravel road had many mud holes, and was not the route of choice at this time of the year. Moreover it was crossed by a number of logging roads, and at each of these the van slowed down, and Corporal Dodds would look one way and the constable the other and simultaneously give the clear signal with upraised thumbs.

From previous experience in the military, I had a distinct impression that such military precision and efficiency was often followed by a monumental debacle, and my spirits were not raised by seeing it demonstrated again in civilian life.

Low clouds hung about with half a moon, which gave little light. Half way to Kitwanga the van lurched into a mud hole deeper than usual and stuck fast. This was the signal for excess bodies to get out and push. Corporal Dodds, reminding us that a driver was not a helper, roared the engine and alternated between forward and reverse gears. The passengers, the constable and me, were by definition pushers. We leaned into the rear fenders and pushed. The spinning wheels covered us with wet and icy mud, and finally the van crawled forward out of the hole and on its way.

It was not a very cheery crew that arrived at the flats adjacent to Kitwanga. A low river mist spread three feet deep above the ground, resulting in an eerie scene. The top halves of villagers seemed to float above the mist, while from the waist down they were obscured.

The three of us stiffly got out of the van, wet and uncomfortable, and Corporal Dodds asked loudly for someone to lead us to Oscar. Sure enough, we were led to a spot ten metres off the road to find our gunshot victim lying flat, shivering with the cold, and groaning in his misery. Corporal Dodds said, "Okay, Doc, better have a look at him before we move him."

I approached Oscar and offered some comforting words such as, "All right Oscar, we're here to make sure that you get the best care. Just relax while I check this." As I said this I noticed a short-barrelled .22 rifle flung to the side. Oscar lay still and in spite of the groans, seemed to be breathing regularly. By flash light I found a cold hand and wrist with a pulse strong and regular. While the whole village had come out to surround Oscar, no one had thought to put a blanket over him to keep him warm.

My attention was drawn to a stained area on the front of his shirt where blood oozed in a widening circle. This finding was ominous. With a catch in my voice, I repeated soothing words to Oscar to the effect that he was in good hands, and all would be well. This comforted him more than it reassured me, and the moaning and groaning stopped even as the silent onlookers breathed a little easier.

In spite of the cold, I unbuttoned Oscar's coat, undid his shirt buttons, and examined his chest more closely. Sure enough, there

Oscar was formed lying on ground at Kitwanga Flats.

was a bullet hole entering his chest over his heart. A thin streak of blood trickled over the whitened skin. I was about to tell Corporal Dodds that the situation did not look good when I searched a bit further. About one inch from the entrance wound of the bullet was a blue, round exit wound. The bullet had simply gone through the skin of his chest, coursed laterally, and exited again. It was a very superficial wound indeed, without any life-threatening possibilities.

My concern and compassion disappeared. In its place came annoyance, weariness, and a sense of being used. Instead of a pleasant evening with wife and child I had the inconvenience of pushing a two-ton vehicle in the mud, and of a thirty mile trip each way through a rough and muddy backwoods road.

"Oscar," I said, "get up on your feet."

Oscar, startled, leaped to his feet amid a scattering of "Ooohs" and "Aaahs" from the astounded onlookers.

The three of us, with Oscar in the back seat, made our way back to the Hazelton hospital over the previously endured, indescribably bad road. On our arrival at the hospital a chest x-ray was done, band-aids applied to two wounds in the chest wall, and Oscar was given a sedative, and sent to bed where he promptly fell asleep.

Tongue in cheek, Corporal Dodds remarked that, since I had resurrected Oscar, could I give a further demonstration and perhaps walk on water?

Be that as it may, I'll never forget the response of the villagers, the "Ooohs" and "Aaahs" when on Kitwanga flats I commanded Oscar to get up on his feet, and, like Lazarus of old, he arose and walked.

CHAPTER 20

THE STORY OF WHISPERING WILLY

The relationship between the medical practitioners and the RCMP was always cordial, but between myself and Whispering Willy there was a particular friendship, based in part on mutual respect for each other's role in the community, plus appreciation of the other's humorous approach to frailties that beset humanity.

Willy Dodds was an old-fashioned cop. He had gained his early experience in the British Columbia Provincial Police Force, then joined the RCMP at forty when the Mounties took over provincial duties. He had a sturdy frame, was 5'10", weighed 240 pounds, and most of this was muscle. His face was rounded, colour high, and he came by his nickname Whispering Willy from the fact that his voice at its lowest volume could be heard forty yards away. His normal voice was audible a full block. No one had ever heard him yell, but it probably would have resounded between Hazelton and Kispiox some ten miles distant.

I first met Whispering Willy when he came to my office with a two centimetre cut on the back of his thumb. I'm not sure how he received this, but I'm reasonably certain that it wasn't in the line of duty, and I suspected that it was in helping his wife peel the potatoes. I put in local freezing and a couple of stitches and congratulated Willy on enduring such a minor wound without fainting. Willy snorted in disgust and reminded me that in a soft job like mine there weren't many events warranting fainting.

I reminded him, "Look Willy, in my day I spent some time in the commandos, and these guys didn't come wimping around to see the MO for a little nick. Anything short of a slash on the jugular was treated with a band-aid."

This occasioned a good deal of humorous exchange about the relative toughness of soldiers and the Mounties, and finally Willy said, "Look, I'll show you. Hit me in the stomach."

I said, "Willy, if I hit a cop in the stomach, it's good for two years in the cooler. If I spend two years in the cooler, who's going to look after your mosquito bites?"

Willy said, "Oh, don't be a wimp, and I'll show you something about being tough."

Finally, with some persuasion, I leaned back and came forward with a solid blow to his stomach with a peculiar little twist that I had learned about hand-to-hand combat.

Willy didn't even grunt, but I could tell that for a fleeting moment there was a pained expression. As for my hand, it felt like it had hit a brick wall, and I stood there wringing my injured right knuckles. At that we called it a day, I wasn't invited to hit him in the middle again, and I didn't risk my scalpel-wielding hand either.

Whispering Willy had a good appreciation of what was required of a commanding officer in a small detachment of the RCMP. He realized that not only was justice necessary, but it had to seem to be accomplished. Once early in my practice, he came to me with a troubled look. "Your friend George up in Two Mile is bootlegging moonshine, and I'm going to have to bust him if he doesn't stop." Willy knew that George was having a good deal of trouble financially, and this comment was Willy's way of sending an unofficial warning. Soon after I saw George for the treatment of a minor condition, and as delicately as possible, I brought up the matter of the outside activities. He did not seem to be startled, but he was troubled.

I asked what the problem was, and he mentioned that he had recently lost his wife from cancer. Apparently she had developed breast cancer, and in spite of his being a carpenter with intermittent employment, he had sent her to the best and most expensive surgeon in Vancouver. The surgery cost over $5,000, and he was paying it off at $100 a month. Since his income was very meagre, he had to supplement it to make these payments. The sale of off-premise alcohol was his one source of extra income. I sympathized with him. Basically a decent person, George certainly believed in paying his debts. To worsen the tragedy, his wife lived only two years after the surgery, and he still had two years of payments to make.

I spoke quite firmly to him and said, "I know that it's important to you to pay your doctor and show your appreciation for his care, but it's also important to obey the law. I'll smooth things over with the police, and you stop breaking the law, and do the best you can with your surgeon in Vancouver."

Quietly I got back to Corporal Dodds, and told him that any alleged activity by my friend George, which I was not admitting, would cease forthwith, and he nodded in appreciation.

Willy had three constables underneath him, and often these were inexperienced. He gave a firm dictum to his constables. They were not to get into fights when enforcing of the law. If they needed help, they were to call for it and back away from exchanging blows. Reinforcement was not always easily available, since, while the Mounties always got their man, they sometimes needed a rest from the pursuit. It so happened that one of his likeable, young constables, in attempting to arrest an abrasive tough, got into an outright altercation which resulted in his being pummelled to the ground.

Willy was furious. He walked down the darkened street and met the bouncer who was telling his friends how he had decked a Mountie. Willy hit him one blow and knocked him flat, picked up one of his heels, dragged him the 100 yards to the detachment quarters, and threw him into the cell. His young Mountie was sent up to the hospital with a friendly passer-by, and Willy took over the rest of the night duties himself.

Next morning, the bruised and battered young constable was given a stern lecture and sent home for a day or two of rest. Willy also gave a short lecture to the repentant offender who had spent the night in the cell. "I pulled that punch, so I didn't hit you hard, but let me tell you, if you ever cause more trouble in this town, you'll wish you were hit by a train rather than me. Now get out and stay out." As far I know this was a lesson that did not need repeating.

Very little went on in the community that either Willy or I was not aware of. At that time a young couple in their twenties, married for approximately two years, lived on the main thoroughfare through Two Mile. It was noted and remarked on that an RCMP vehicle was seen parked either beside or close to their house during the night. It was also noticed that this occurred only when the husband was away working on construction jobs.

I knew that the husband was basically a decent sort, hard-working and serious. His wife was a full-figured, bold girl, who managed to wear her blouse with an extra button undone, always a bit lower than most respectable women. From visits in the clinic I knew that she was less than happy with limited activity when her husband was home and the lights were doused.

Finally the whispers and gossip could no longer be ignored. I took Willy aside and mentioned what a noble thing that the Mounties were about, bringing joy and gladness to the hearts of lonely females in the community.

Willy cocked his head at an angle and said, "It's that young Joe and Julie, isn't it?"

I said, "I don't think we can ignore it any longer, Willy, and it's going to cause problems in this community if something isn't done."

Willy said, "Leave the matter with me," and the next thing I heard was that young Constable Joe had been transferred so far north he had to look over his shoulder to see Canada. Marital fidelity returned to Julie and her husband, but I continued to note frustration and dissatisfaction in her eye. Likely, in the long run, it boded ill for them.

The easy, friendly relationship between Whispering Willy and myself continued over my two years in Hazelton. We dealt with assaults, pedophiles, robberies, murder, gunshot wounds, sexual abuse, automobile accidents, and riots with, I think, a reasonable amount of efficiency and humanity.

It was a human weakness that led to Willy's undoing. When he was posted in Hazelton, a rumour persisted that his wife abused alcohol. She had had several minor car accidents, and on occasion appeared to be intoxicated. I suspected a good part of their income was spent on alcohol by the time they left Hazelton.

In those days, Mounties were transferred regularly, and one day Willy Dodd and his alcoholic wife left Hazelton behind. At Willy's next posting a cache of booze was seized from bootleggers, and in a moment of foolishness, Willy took the bottles home to supply his wife's habit.

Caught and busted, he would never have an RCMP detachment again. Humiliated and broken, he was transferred to guard duty at a government building in Victoria and finished his career with a cloud over his head. I often think of Willy, knowing he was one good cop.

CHAPTER 21

THE SAGA OF ADANAS PETE

This story has a moral, an important one, for it shows that there is more than one way to get to heaven.

In my second year at Hazelton it was noted that much time had passed since a distant Native village had been visited for medical care. Accordingly, a party composed of the Indian agent, a nurse and me still fresh from the halls of learning, left Hazelton by float plane, bound for the remote settlement at the end of Babine Lake.

Our flight was somewhat harrowing until we safely landed. The float plane taxied to the beach, where we were met by a flock of chattering Native children. All were soon happily chewing on candies supplied from the Indian agent's voluminous pockets.

Babine Village consisted of a number of houses clustered along the lake and up the hill. A large Catholic church, complete with a huge bell, was located near the shore. Opposite the church was the Hudson's Bay Trading Post and a school with living quarters attached.

We were soon settled into the teacher's quarters which was commodious and comfortable, but had only two bedrooms for the three of us. I suggested that the doctor and nurse share one room, since their actions were surely above reproach. This motion was vetoed and instead, I found myself sharing a room with the Indian agent, a man with considerable knowledge of the local natives and their history.

The Carrier Natives of British Columbia were essentially a Stone Age people until the coming of the white man. They had no metal instruments, little medicine, no agriculture, and the only domesticated animal was a small breed of dog. Their language is an Athabascan dialect spoken across northern Canada to Ontario and in two isolated areas in Nevada and Arizona. Their food was wild game and the plentiful salmon which came up the river. The people of this village were improvident and never seemed to get enough dried salmon put away to last the winter; spring usually found them hungry, if not starving.

The name 'Carrier' came from the tribal custom of cremating the dead. The wife of a deceased man was required to carry his ashes on her back. If she was suspected of being inattentive before her husband's death, relatives of the dead husband made sure that she came very near the flames during the burning. In the old days it was not uncommon for wives to hang themselves rather than go through the ceremony.

The morning after our arrival I held a clinic in the classroom of the school. Many people came, most just to see the new doctor. The nurse had a great fund of knowledge about the village and seemed to know each person's name, relationship, as well as their medical history. We saw a number of minor illnesses such as infections, rheumatism, unhealed wounds, and of course, decayed teeth. With one ancient pair of forceps and plentiful local anesthetic, I was able to extract no less then twelve rotten teeth.

The clinic hours went quickly, and at the end I was left with one-round faced man who happily told me his name was Adanas Pete. He was full of stories of the village and the people, and I took

the opportunity to ask him why the people, who lived by a great lake, could not swim. His explanation gave me a good deal of insight into the tribal philosophy. Said he, "A man is out in the big lake, and his canoe sinks. If he is able to swim, he swims, and he swims, and no matter how good a swimmer he is, he can't make it to shore, and he drowns. Better he drown by his canoe!"

That afternoon four of us drifted down the river flowing from the lake and fished for trout and whitefish. The angling was good, and after a few hours we had twenty or thirty plump fish. As we floated peacefully the silence was broken by the roar of a motor boat rapidly coming down the river. It made a wide circle around us and stopped close by. The young boatman shouted loudly, "Doctor, come quickly — Adanas Pete has shot himself!"

Our guide looked dubious and remarked that someone was always shooting himself and never seemed to do much damage. However, something in the young man's voice made me pull in my rod. The others did likewise, and we hurried back to the settlement. I stopped to pick up my medical bag and proceeded into the Indian village. Around the house furthest up the slope, a crowd had gathered and stood waiting silently. I made my way to the door, where the chief and an elder blocked the entry.

"Are you the doctor?" asked the chief.

"Yes."

"All right, you go in."

He opened the door and I slipped inside. The house was typical for this village. There was one large room, with iron cots on each side and a stove on the far end. In the middle was a table with loaves of freshly baked bread and a pot of boiled salmon.

On a bed at the other end of the room sat Adanas Pete with his head peacefully slumped onto his knees. Beside him was a short .22 calibre rifle, and it was quite apparent he had departed from this world. I was baffled to find the cause of his death, until I happened to look behind his left ear, and there found a small hole, surrounded by specks of powder burn. No medical attention was going to help him, so I made my way back to the door. As I emerged from the building, the chief looked at me inquiringly and said, "How is our brother?"

"Chief, our brother is not very well," I said. "In fact, he is dead."

In a tranquil village on Babine Lake, Eldon encountered both tragedy and an unusual outcome. (Courtesy Dr Rob McGuiness)

At these words, which seemed to be telegraphed immediately to everyone assembled, pandemonium broke loose. People screamed and wailed and tore at their hair. Someone ran to the church and rang the bell thunderously. Dogs barked, children cried, and everything was in a complete uproar. One woman in particular was screaming and throwing herself about in an alarming fashion. Thinking she was the wife of Adanas, I was about to give her a sedative, when the chief caught my eye and shook his head. Apparently she was paid to wail and lament.

Dinner that night was sober in spite of excellent fried trout, which the health nurse had prepared. Midway through the meal we were interrupted by the arrival of the Roman Catholic priest, Father Connolly, who had hiked in twenty miles from a neighboring lake.

The conversation turned to the sad events of the day. I was startled to hear Father Connolly state that Adanas Pete, because of the manner of his death, could not be buried in the village cemetery. Suicide was becoming a ritual here, he claimed, and every big community event presented the danger of being marred by the suicide of someone seeking notoriety. In vain I argued that Adanas Pete had been a good man and only committed suicide because his thinking was muddled by alcohol. Father Connolly was firm; Adanas Pete could not be buried in the graveyard.

The faces of the kin of Adanas Pete were dark and sullen as he was laid to rest in unconsecrated ground. Although it was outside the boundary, they had dug the grave only inches from the fence, as close to the graveyard as it was possible to place him.

We returned to Hazelton. Autumn leaves changed to winter snow, and the wind whistled dolefully across the lonely grave. It was said that the soul of Adanas Pete, estranged from the heaven-bound brothers, was heard to cry in the long nights of darkness.

A few years later I happened to meet Father Connolly again, and we fell into friendly recollection of our previous encounter. We were about to part when he asked, "Did you hear the final outcome of the Adanas Pete affair?" He chuckled ruefully. Two years after the event Father Connolly and his bishop chanced to return to the Babine village. There they were met by an assembly of elders who asked for a private meeting with the bishop. Father Connolly offered to interpret, but the Natives insisted they must see the bishop in private.

On their return home, Father Connolly was bursting with curiosity and finally asked the bishop what could be so important that the elders required a private audience. The bishop replied that it had turned out to be not a very important matter. The Natives felt their graveyard too small, and at their request he had consecrated an additional piece of ground.

The very next day the Carriers of Babine Lake had a great work party and moved their cemetery fence. In fact, they expanded the graveyard a total of five feet along one side. Inside the boundary of the newly consecrated ground was one additional grave. You guessed it, the grave of Adanas Pete!

CHAPTER 22

MY FRIENDS
DONALD AND MARY GRAY

During my two years of practice in Hazelton, I became acquainted with almost every individual in the area. Some, because of their unique and delightful personalities, have remained in my memory through the years. One couple, Donald and Mary Gray, was a special joy to me.

Donald and Mary were Carrier, whose first language was Athabascan. Chinook and English were secondary. They lived in a frame house by the road at Hagwilget on the west side of the Bulkley river between New Hazelton and Old Hazelton. They were both in their 70s when I knew them. Donald, of slender build, was tall for a native at 5'10" and stooped at the shoulder. His woolen trousers were

Mary and Donald Gray.

matched with a soft checkered shirt which he left unbuttoned at the top, his undershirt showing through. Mary was shorter than Donald and of medium build; she wore a plain dress and knit woolen sweater. They were often seen walking together either to New Hazelton, or returning to Hagwilget with their weekly supply of groceries.

I first met Donald during a busy afternoon office practice. After reviewing his medical chart I found that his main complaint was of arthritis. I expected to give him some aspirin and perhaps some analgesics and have him away in five minutes. Our exchange, I learned, was not to be approached in an abrupt manner, and our conversation started by reviewing the condition of the weather and the fishing run, the expected growth of their vegetable garden as compared with the past years, and then on to serious things which might trouble him health-wise.

At the conclusion of the visit, I said goodbye and Donald said, "Doctor, I play for you."

I saw no musical instrument, but I understood the Carrier difficulty with the letter "r", and realised that he wished to pray for me. Knowing a doctor needs all the prayer possible, I stood up also, and Donald began speaking with eloquence and reverence.

Immediately I recognized this was a prayer to which the Almighty would pay careful attention; the richness and sincerity of Donald's voice filled the office.

Salmon drying and smoke house. The smell and flies were inde-scribable.

He began with a general prayer for peace, for people and provision for their needs. Then, raising his voice, prayer for special blessing for our leaders, for their wisdom and greater attention to the needs of people of which they may have been a bit forgetful in the past.

At this time I was able to hear hints of my office nurse's restlessness. She rustled papers and frequently visited the closed office door.

Donald paid no heed whatsoever, and proceeded on in an orderly fashion, bringing to God's attention all the nurses by name and the doctors, his friends, the Catholic priest, the local United Church minister, the teachers, and with some lesser enthusiasm, members of the local police force.

At this time there was no mistaking that my office nurse was becoming impatient, but Donald was not distracted one bit. Finally after fifteen or twenty minutes, he finished with a grand, eloquent finale, "Oh Lord, your humble and faithful servants all look forward to that great day when all of us good Catholics shall be gathered together with you in heaven."

Stout Presbyterian as I was, I could not help but say, "Amen, Donald, we all look forward to that great day. Give my kind regards to Mary, and come back in a month's time."

Donald returned again and again. Monthly I was sure that the complaints would be the similar, the treatment consistent with the medical findings, and the prayer as sincere and as lengthy as the original. I always felt, however, that the Almighty listened carefully to Donald and never begrudged him the office time even though my nurse seemed to become more impatient with each visit.

Somewhere along in the relationship I came to a greater understanding of the Chinook language. When Donald or Mary spoke to me it was either in English with some Chinook words, or sometimes straight Chinook. They never spoke to me in their native Athabascan language, which was almost beyond the learning capacity of white occidentals. Indeed, Donald could not speak the language of the people 300 yards away across the river who spoke Tsimshian, an entirely different language. Communications between the two peoples used Chinook or English.

The Chinook language was a fascinating mode of communication. Apparently, before the white man came to the Pacific, a language was used between different peoples, extending from Oregon to Alaska,

Opposite: Mary Gray at a salmon drying shed.

and from the Pacific coast to Alberta. When the white people came, the language became known as Chinook, and was simply enlarged to include a number of English words, as well as French. When a few Chinese words were incorporated into the lingua franca, lo and behold, there was a language which could be spoken throughout the whole area.

This language remained common until about 1960, and indeed, many courts of law had a Chinook translator. There were perhaps 2500 distinct words in the language, and there were no tenses, definite articles, genders, or plurals. The finer points of communication were imparted by adding more Chinook words to the sentence.

My knowledge of Chinook pleased Donald, and we would hold more or less intelligible conversation in this jargon. I would say, "*Kloshe tenas sun. Klahowya* Donald," which means, "Good morning, Donald. How are you?" Donald would reply, "Very well, my friend. *Hiyu kloshe nesika schik docto klenih mika.* And how are you, my doctor?"

The common bonds of language and attitude gave us an easy familiarity and I came to know some of the circumstances governing their lives. Donald and Mary were devout Catholics, but their children had a very loose attachment to their church, and respected neither their Carrier beliefs nor the Christian church that meant so much to their parents. Donald and Mary clung to their past pattern of life in

that they hunted and fished and planted their garden. Their children were more attuned to five working days and corn flakes and white flour. The production of oil in the Mid-East was as important to them as were dog teams and pack horses to Donald and Mary. In addition, the scourge of alcohol and in some instances other substances beset the younger generation. These were vices to which Donald and Mary were essentially immune, although on occasion Mary sat on their porch smoking a straight stemmed pipe.

Close to the end of my time at Hazelton, I was called to their home to visit Mary, who was doing poorly, according to Donald. I had heard rumours that her health was failing, but had not seen Mary in my office for months. I found her propped up in bed looking worn and ill. Underneath her was a worn mattress, and over her one single woolen blanket. A couple of pillows propped her shoulders, and I was

immediately suspicious of heart failure. This was confirmed by finding swollen feet, congested lungs, and an irregular heart-beat.

"Donald," I said, "we must take Mary to hospital." He demurred, "Doctor, first we must have tea." He busied himself heating water on the wood burning stove, then cut thick slices of home-made bread, serving them with butter and home-made saskatoon berry jam. After tea we helped Mary into the back seat of my car, and drove to the hospital.

Mary's condition was far advanced, and in spite of treatment, she never left her hospital bed. Donald was in constant attendance, waiting on Mary, and at night pulled a mattress from one of the other beds of the ward, and slept on the floor beside her.

At the end, I touched my friend on the shoulder and told him that Mary was gone.

Donald stood up and said simply, "*Yaka kopa saghalie illahie nesika klotchman.*" That is, "My wife is in heaven, *kopa saghalie tyee*, with God."

With tears I replied, "*Mary kopa saghalie tyee.*" "Mary is with God."

Donald took my hand and said, "Doctor, I play for you." In spite of my sadness I could not help but listen for the ending, and sure enough it was there. "Oh Lord, we look forward to that great day when all good Catholics are joined together with you in heaven."

I said, "Amen, even so do we all."

Salmon drying shed in Hagwilget.
The totems are of past good fishing.

CHAPTER 23

TIMES THAT TRY
THE HEARTS OF DOCTORS

Medical practice in Hazelton held an even pace for the most part. There was a steady occurrence of respiratory infections, minor surgery, a few fractures, and other infections, but serious emergency complications were quite rare.

The two most traumatic involved babies, one eighteen months old and the other a premature newborn. The toddler was a native boy, the only child of a couple, both in their thirties, the wife older than the husband. They had been infertile through their married life, and the young boy was adopted, and of mixed parentage. Because of these circumstances the adoptive parents tended to be anxious and insecure, and I was not particularly worried when they telephoned late one afternoon to express anxiety about the child.

They brought the boy to an outpatient clinic. He did not look terribly ill, but did show signs of departure from his usual, chubby, healthy self. His temperature was elevated to 100° F, his colour high, and he was cranky and irritable; these symptoms often appear in an infant with an upper respiratory infection or infection of the ears. Laboratory tests seemed to confirm an inflammatory process, and since fluid intake was marginal, he was admitted to hospital and intravenous fluids were started with systemic antibiotics. For good measure I asked Dr Palmer to see the infant, and a call was made to a pediatrician in Vancouver General Hospital.

As the malady persisted, the parents became more and more worried. One or the other was at the side of the child through the night. The day after admission the child was decidedly worse. His abdomen was bloated, his temperature elevated to 103° F, his neck stiff and his cry high-pitched.

At this point a test was done, which in retrospect should have been done earlier; this test was a spinal tap. The result confirmed our worst fears — the child had meningitis, or infection of the spinal cord. The spinal fluid, which normally should be clear, was clouded, and microscopic examination showed it was loaded with pus cells. Further tests did not show active bacteria, likely due to the antibiotic usage, or otherwise suggesting that the organism was not bacterial but either viral or tuberculous.

As the attending physician I felt guilt-stricken, and carried a burden almost greater than I was able to bear. The parents were frantic with grief and worry, and their emotions were easily transferred into anger against the medical staff and the nurses.

In spite of intense and constant medical care, the infant died on the third day. There was no effective way of consoling the adoptive parents. Concerned neighbours and friends kept a constant vigil with them, but provided no real solace to sway their grief.

The little boy was buried one day later. Harold Gould, our maintenance supervisor, made a small coffin of pine boards.

I did not attend the funeral, which was conducted by our kindly, elderly minister and his wife, but I was informed of the heart-rending details. The parents sobbed and screamed throughout the service, and when the body of the child was laid in the ground, the mother tried to fling herself into the open grave.

Experiences like this are difficult to forget. The thought, "If only I had performed this test earlier, or used a different treatment," ran through the minds of the doctors involved. The results were tragic and disastrous. The child was dead, the burden of grief and guilt wrecked the marriage, and the couple separated and moved from the community. As doctors, we had to accept that we were not God, we were fallible, and in this fallibility may be seeds of human tragedy. Still, there was much soul-searching, and a weighing of good things accomplished against the rare sad outcome. No amount of money would ever compensate a medical doctor for the turmoil and anguish occasioned by an experience such as this.

The second most traumatic clinical experience came on the maternity floor. Normally childbirth is a happy time, but with serious complications, it is as if the roof had fallen in. The second-worst news for a doctor to deliver is to tell young parents that there will be no baby to bring home. The only thing worse is to inform a young husband that there will be no child and no wife either, both having died in the childbirth process.

A series of tragic events arose following a seemingly innocuous telephone call one evening at Wrinch Memorial. The call was from June, a young mother with three children, now in the seventh month of her fourth pregnancy. She informed me that she was experiencing some minor bleeding.

Now bleeding at this stage of pregnancy can be harmless or can be most serious. June was advised to report to the hospital immediately, and shortly afterwards arrived in the back of a van. The slight bleeding had increased considerably on her admission to hospital. Examination confirmed that the pregnancy was approximately three months from her due date, and the infant was alive and apparently well.

An intravenous was started and two units of blood, typed and crossed, held in reserve. At approximately eleven o'clock at night June rang to the nurse, and the moderately heavy bleeding had become major hemorrhage. The two units of blood were started immediately, but with only 1000 cc's of blood, there was no chance of replacing the quantity lost. We were fortunate to have on duty two nurses who were O Rh negative, which is a universal donor blood type. They were called into hospital and a generous pint of blood taken from each. At this point we were still at least two quarts of blood behind the loss, and June, attempting to sit up in bed, passed a large blood clot. Forgetting formalities she said, "Eldon, I think I'm going to die."

I replied, "Hold on, June, you're not going to die."

We immediately put two of the other staff who had June's blood type on stretchers and took two more pints of blood from them, and transferred them to the patient.

At this point the hemorrhage continued, and June was in shock. Worst of all, we had no further bottles for collecting blood, and the nearest supply was in Smithers, forty miles away.

June's husband was the local taxi operator, and the best suited to drive to Smithers and bring back blood collecting units, so we dispatched him into the night.

It was obvious that June's baby had to be delivered. We took June to the operating room, and in spite of the shock and loss of blood, a Caesarean section was done under local freezing.

I had performed perhaps a dozen C-sections during my short career and was delegated to do the surgery. Somehow I managed a

Caesarean section under these most adverse circumstances. June still bled heavily, but a small female infant was delivered and the diagnosis of misplaced afterbirth confirmed. Surprisingly, even with this massive hemorrhage the infant was still alive and gave a feeble cry at delivery. Somehow the incision into the uterus was sutured and the abdominal wall brought back together. June remained alive by the narrowest of margins.

The infant, grossly premature, survived for an hour only. By the time her husband returned, June had stabilized, and we counted ourselves lucky to have a mother still with us, in spite of the loss of her baby. June and her husband went on to have further healthy babies, and could never show enough their gratitude for the heroic efforts we had made.

In these times of terrible stress, doctors could well question their devotion and loyalty to the discipline imposed by the profession of medicine; discipline handed down from Hippocrates himself 2400 years ago.

This credo demands responsibility but, in times of trial, also delivers comfort and strength, often enabling the doctor to endure.

CHAPTER 24

A SUBSTANTIAL PRESERVE IN THE COMMUNITY

Doctors are held in high regard in smaller communities. This regard was perhaps stronger in the past than in the present age of high tech treatments, but in times past the doctor was one of the more prominent members of the community, ranking with the clergy, town councillors, and high school principals.

Coming to Hazelton for my first medical position, this role was new for me, and for Marjorie, who shared it. Prior to that time I enjoyed a certain prestige involved in my rank in the hierarchy of major hospitals, but Marjorie and I had little impact on the community around us. In Hazelton our judgement often meant life and death decisions, the birth of newborn babies and the final care to the dying.

Once sound judgement was demonstrated, the doctor and his family were taken into people's hearts and automatically included in most social functions and matters of civic concern. Our opinions were sought by people with much more knowledge in a given field than our own and given weighty consideration, whether we knew anything about the matter or not. Marjorie and I soon mastered the art of being courteous and receptive to other's feelings and opinions without venturing into fields of which we had no knowledge.

I learned the value of tact the hard way, after I responded frankly when asked to express my opinion during a school board meeting. As it turned out, my opinion was at odds with those of almost all the others present, and at the conclusion, they shuttled me out with more courtesy than appreciation. Still Marjorie and I took to the community, and the community took to us.

I loved animals and after hours from my medical practice enjoyed opportunities to give help and advice in the veterinary field, ranging from surgery on cats and dogs to learned discourses on ailing budgies. One Sunday afternoon, a distraught family brought their small dog to the hospital. It had been hit by a car, and its hind leg was horribly fractured, with the bone protruding through the skin.

I took one look at the animal, which was obviously in pain, and tried to comfort the family. I advised them that the best course was to put the animal down. When I said this, there were loud wails and tears from all the children and wringing of hands from the parents. Finally, against my better advice, I yielded to their entreaties, gave the dog a sedative and then sprayed on ethyl chloride which produces almost immediate anaesthesia. The leg was then amputated, skin ends brought over the stump, and after a hefty shot of antibiotics the animal was sent home. Much to my surprise, three weeks later the family came back with their dog which was happily making its way on three legs and keeping up with the cheerful, laughing children.

Marjorie, being a Salvation Army officer's daughter, took over the Canadian Girls In Training (CGIT) and we both led a co-ed teenage group. One famous event was titled, "Beans for Teens" and featured a chili and hamburger supper. It received good attendance from all segments of the community.

A doctors wife had many responsibilities. Marjorie far left, back row, led this CGIT group of seven. She was also pregnant with our second child at the time.

Marjorie, with our one-year old first boy, and pregnant with our second child was always a source of advice on child-rearing for young mothers who were often far away from parental and family support.

I took it upon myself to coach the hospital girls' softball team. We were very successful, but I made a few blunders, such as suggesting that our catcher move closer to the plate than her usual distance of fifteen feet. No sooner had she moved up than the first pitch came whistling in from the pitcher and caught her full in the face. She promptly resigned as first catcher and our team's record went down a notch.

I enjoyed taking part in pick-up baseball and hockey matches and games and to some extent proved to be a stabilizing element and example to the young people.

When our hospital maintenance man's son found high school a burden and decided to enlist in the air force, I gave him the best advice about the armed forces that I knew. This was to think what he wanted, but say only what was prudent. My advice apparently worked for him, because he ended up twenty-five years later a major, well respected.

In the social life at the hospital grounds we found ourselves included in almost all the youth activities. We were the youngest doctor and wife and found ourselves involved in the amusements and activities of the nurses and their boyfriends. A Native game called "a lahal" always created howls of merriment. Everyone sat on the floor in a ring, and a bone was passed behind the backs of the players. When a drummer stopped, the player in the middle attempted to choose who held the bone. Of course, in the movement of the stick behind backs there was a good deal of nudging and squeezing and pushing and flirting, and for all I know, pinching as well.

The great triumph of our hospital staff was in the presentation of the operetta Carmen at the community's spring talent show. Of course we had to have a bull, toreador, a gypsy girl, and for one scene, a multitude of spectators around the bull ring.

Our maintenance supervisor, Harold Gould, made a bull from paper maché with genuine horns. The nurses painted more or less realistic Spaniards on broad sheets of wall paper; the local dance instructor, Thyra, organized the choreography and a little, dark-haired, black-eyed nurse made a perfect Carmen.

Mt Rocher de Boule gave a benediction as we left Hazelton.

To the authentic background music on a gramophone, the play was enacted with such verve and panache that our most prominent local citizen, an amateur thespian, jumped to his chair, waved his scarf, and shouted out, "Olé!" The presentation was a great success, we took top spot, and the bull's head could be seen above the maintenance shop for years after.

When our time came to depart Hazelton, we felt a real sense of loss and sadness. Marjorie, a real trouper from her Salvation Army roots, could not help but break down and weep torrents as we took our final leave.

Two miles down the road on our departure, Mary and Allan Benson hailed us down and took us into their home for a final good-bye. Mary made the best pies in the world, and had banana cream, strawberry, and lemon. At her insistence we had a piece from each and the memory warms us still.

Further down the road we had to stop and say goodbye one last time to old Donald Gray at Hagwilget. Never did we leave an area with such a feeling of having bonded with the community. Hazelton, distinct, unique, at times awkward, we truly fell in love with you.

CHAPTER 25

Kos At Last

Two years after I arrived at Hazelton as an untried doctor, I paused to reflect on my accomplishments. I had an inner sense of satisfaction that I had become a competent practitioner. I had successfully dealt with complicated births, diagnostic puzzles, challenging crises, and sometimes, as patients faced the inevitable, a protracted time of dying. In confronting these events I acquired a maturity of judgement and an equanimity that could not easily be upset.

Marjorie and I had developed as substantial citizens in the community, and to a degree had refined some of the social skills necessary for our role. We were now young parents involved in raising and providing for our two children, with expectations of a third.

I reflected back on the many patients who had been helped by my medical care and also thought of those who had been instrumental in furthering my knowledge and skills as a doctor.

June came into my mind, and involuntarily my heart raced. On that one night June had stressed me to the limit, and came within a breath of dying. Teamwork resulted in a young mother's life being saved. I thought of a fatal meningitis, and Thomas who broke his neck and lost his life from a runaway team and wagon accident, of the women who died from that cruelest of diseases, breast cancer.

The pluck and courage of Hazelton's two young Salvation Army women never ceased to amaze me and I learned much from their faithfulness in the midst of troubled times and social stresses. The battle of the one young woman with Guillain-Barré syndrome taught me a lesson in humility. Sometimes the afflictions besetting our human body can confound the wisest of medical minds. The real characters of the community made me pause sometimes in frustration, sometimes in admiration, sometimes in a good-humoured chuckle. Whispering Willy, Donald and Mary Gray were the spice in my life.

Some characters, I have chosen not to dwell on — like Scotty Mac, a rogue who invaded the genetic pool in assorted villages with great success. I thought with an involuntary shudder of Joe, a little boy without many friends in this world, who took it upon himself to wander out of the hospital, barefoot, on a cold wintery night. Doctors were helpless and frantic and then rejoiced with the hermit saviour.

All of these experiences when taken in isolation were built into a structure for my future life in medicine, a foundation that was a solid as the undergirding of a castle.

The oath of Hippocrates of the Greek isle of Kos has been taken by doctors for over 2000 years, and was an oath that I solemnly swore to uphold on graduation from medical school. It goes as follows: "By Apollo, the physician, I swear to teach my fellow practitioner and regard him as myself, to keep the welfare of patients always foremost, and above all do no harm, to refrain from seduction of people under my care in their household, to avoid the poisons, and to do no abortions, nor harm to any living individual." After these all came the warning. If I should be unfaithful to these vows, the worst of ill times were to be my lot.

From Cariboo to Kos I had made the symbolic journey from a simple pastoral occupation to a respected position worthy of Hippocrates. The father of modern medicine, in my odyssey, had been reaffirmed.

From Kos, Hippocrates had journeyed forth. Was it to great things? Was Hazelton a torch to light my own path to greater things? Time would tell.

PIONEER VOICES SERIES

A WORD ABOUT THE HERITAGE HOUSE PIONEER VOICES SERIES

A Western Doctor's Odyssey is the latest offering in the Heritage House series of first-person accounts of frontier life in Western Canada and the Pacific Northwest. This collection of books explores the lives and accomplishments of men and women who epitomize the pioneer spirit and resilience that characterizes this country. All books include a blend of personal and archival photos. They range in length from 64 to 224 pages and in price from $5.95-$17.95.

Other recent titles in this series include:

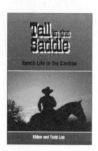   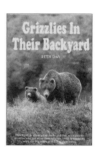

Tall in the Saddle by Eldon and Todd Lee finds two brothers sharing their recollections and observations about growing up on the Hill and Paul Ranch in the Cariboo region of British Columbia. ($14.95)

Totem Poles and Tea by Hughina Herold has been called "an adult version of *Anne of Green Gables*" and a "must-read for all BCers" by independent reviewers. It is an enlightning story of a young nurse- teacher's coming of age in a remote 1930s native village. ($17.95)

Tales of a Pioneer Journalist by David W. Higgins brings alive 18th century life from San Francisco to the BC gold rushes. Written around 1900 by one of the era's most colorful journalists, he entertains and informs his readers with a style deemed by a reviewer as "un-put-downable". ($16.95)

Grizzlies in Their Backyard by Beth Day records the exodus of Jim and Laurette Stanton as they depart Seattle in 1945. In a rowboat powered by a small motor they entered a west coast fiord and spent 30 years living in harmony with the big bears of Knight Inlet. ($14.95)

Doukhobor Daze by Hazel O'Neail is a classic account of a teacher's life in a volatile 1930s western community. There both peaceful and radical arms of a Russian religious sect defined the politics and social boundaries of their new community. ($10.95)

T'shama by Ron Purvis is a native term for "whiteman or authority." Ron was such to a procession of native kids at an Anglican residential school for 14 years and says his "charges crammed a great deal more wisdom into me than I imparted on them." ($5.95)

Cariboo Cowboy by Harry Marriott, written in the 1950s, remains the best of campfire reading for horse and nature lovers throughout the west. The ranch setting at Big Bar Lake captures the soul of cowboy life and the dignity of Harry and Peg Marriott. ($14.95)

March of the Mounties by Sir Cecil Denny is another classic account based on the writings and career of an original Northwest Mounted Police Captain. Later, he became an Indian agent known as "Chief Beaver Coat," a respected rancher and Alberta's Provincial Archivist. ($12.95)

Our Trail Led Northwest by Madge Mandy tells the tales of a petite college teacher joining her new mining engineer, husband, Joe, in 1933, on a trek into the rugged Coast Mountains. Written when she was 88, Madge's tale is both inspiring and evocative.($14.95)

Heritage House Catalogue

A full catalogue of Heritage House books is available by sending mailing costs of $3.00 to #8-17921 55 Ave., Surrey BC, V3S 6C4. The titles noted above and other Heritage House Books are available through most booksellers in Western Canada and the Pacific Northwest and other quality book stores throughout North America.

ABOUT THE AUTHOR

Eldon Lee graduated from the University of Washington Medical School in 1952. He spent his internship and residency years at Vancouver General and Shaughnessy hospitals in Vancouver, British Columbia.

Born in Chico, California in 1923, Eldon was raised with his younger brother, Todd, on a Cariboo ranch before entering military service to become an air force bomber pilot. After completing his medical training, Eldon embarked on his first stint as a rural doctor. With wife Marjorie and their first of six children, the young doctor accepted a position near what was still a frontier of modern life, Hazelton, BC. It is the years spent in that community and the everlasting impressions the people, the environment and diverse medical challenges made on Dr Lee that provide the foundation for this story.

Subsequent to his years in Hazelton, Eldon opted to specialize in obstetrics at Vancouver General, then spent a year as Registrar at Marston Green Maternity Hospital in England. On his return to North America, he again opted to escape big city life and for many years he practised as the only obstetrician and gynecologist in the vast reaches of central BC, north of the fifty-first parallel.

Resident in the community of Prince George for three decades, Eldon Lee is a life member of various medical colleges, associations and societies. He devotes his retirement years to recreational flying, the study of post-graduate Greek, teaching Sunday School and his interest in both fiction and non-fiction writing.

Dr Lee recently celebrated his forty-fourth wedding anniversary with Marjorie and has always recognized the major role she has played in his successful professional life.

In 1995, Eldon co-authored *Tall in the Saddle* with his late brother, Todd, and is currently working on a history of the pioneer doctors of central BC, to be published by Heritage House.

Photo Credits:

Front cover and internal photos have been supplied by the author.
The back cover painting by Emily Carr depicts a grave house at
Hazelton and is from the BC Archives and Records Service collection.